UPLIFT YOUR LIFE

Be a Freelance Consultant and Make a Livelihood and a Life in the New Era of Artificial Intelligence in a Fast-Changing World

SHAHEEL RAFIQUE

ISBN

Hardcase 979-8-89066-716-8
Paperback 979-8-89026-499-2

This book is dedicated to my parents, Monto and Honey, and my children, Alma and Umar.

Contents

Chapter 1

The Future of Work

This book is not the usual kind of book that deals with consulting frameworks, processes, and the art of consulting, or the techniques used in consulting presentations and how one needs to plan and execute a consulting assignment. It attempts to illustrate a wide range of things freelance consultants need to know and the skills needed to be a professional and a good human being. It hopes to help individuals and organizations in the public and private sectors. It attempts to showcase a holistic way of developing oneself as a freelancer.

I see young graduates from MBA and technical schools looking for consulting opportunities, and retired people who feel they already have the skill sets to become consultants, making a fool of themselves in their first assignment or are burnt out by the end of the third. So, I was inspired to write this book for them, so that they can be the best version of themselves in their first assignment as a freelance consultant.

According to the statistics published by Georgi Todorove on April 13, 2023, there are about one billion freelancers in the world. Roughly, 86% of freelancers work from home. It has been estimated that the freelancing industry contributes USD 23.16 to USD 42.9 trillion dollars to the world economy annually.

Around 60% of freelance workers are digital nomads. And 60% of freelancers take around three years to become independent. Around three fourth of the freelancers in the world juggle two to four projects at the same time. Around 70% of freelancers choose this life because of the flexibility in their work and personal growth; only 7% are in it for the money.

Based on earnings, India is one of the fastest-growing freelance markets in the world, with 15 million freelancers in the country. Of these, 80% are men, and 20% are women. India has a freelance year-on-year revenue growth of 160%. The Philippines is however growing the fastest in the world with a year-on-year revenue growth of 208% in 2020.

More than 60% of freelance consultants start freelancing by choice. I became a freelance consultant accidentally, after having to leave a good job in a UN organization due to the usual internal politics and the toxic environment created by untrained managers. However, I was hired by the same organization as their consultant, thanks to the colleagues and friends in the organization who knew me and my work. However, in retrospect, I don't have any regrets; I was pushed into the wonderful world of freelance consulting, which I thoroughly enjoyed.

A statistical survey carried out by *Thrive Myway* shows that 64% of freelancers claim that their mental health has improved since they became freelancers, and 68% of them have reported that their quality of life has improved since they became freelancers.

A freelance consultant works on a contractual basis for a fixed duration, assigned to a project or programme. They are not regular employees and work on short-term contracts lasting for a few days or months, or long-term contracts that last for one to four years. They are usually specialized in one or more skills and have a high level of expertise.

The freelancer brings value to the client and the contracting consulting firm in terms of advice, guidance and professional support. They bring special knowledge and conceptual understanding of the project to the table, which employees of the client organization cannot. They add value, along with other experts, in solving critical problems of the clients, both in the private and public sectors.

Freelancers are paid hourly or daily rates and are responsible for their own invoicing, taxes and other liabilities. They are not entitled to gratuity, pension, annual leave, or other perks which are enjoyed by regular full-time employees, but they earn a lot more, considering the time they invest in the consulting practice with respect to a specific project. Freelancers are well-paid and enjoy considerable freedom and flexibility in their work. They have the option to choose their employer, do what they are good at and grow, and be their own boss. They are sought after because they are highly skilled in their field of expertise.

I believe that freelancing will be a part of the future of work to the extent that people will spend more time working from home and interfacing with Artificial Intelligence (AI) in the rapidly changing world. This book is for those young graduates who have the entrepreneurial spirit to become freelance consultants in any sphere of activity. In addition, this book is also for mid-career executives and those who have retired from public service and private jobs to start a career as a freelancer.

The trend has already been set for freelancing to be a promising career path in the Culture and Creative Industry (CCI). Around 33%

of CCI employees are freelancers. In other subsectors of this industry, freelancers comprise 70% of the workforce.

With the advent of AI, there is a fear that it might replace freelancers very rapidly. This is most unlikely in any field, and even more unlikely to happen in the CCI industry. There is a possibility that in management consulting, most activities related to research and the use of huge data sets will be replaced by AI in terms of data collection, cleaning and analysis. Certain consulting companies have already started using and leveraging the capabilities of AI in terms of natural text editing, automation, and computer vision. Other functions such as automation of operations, marketing and sales and risks are being supported by AI capabilities.

Freelance Consulting is an Art

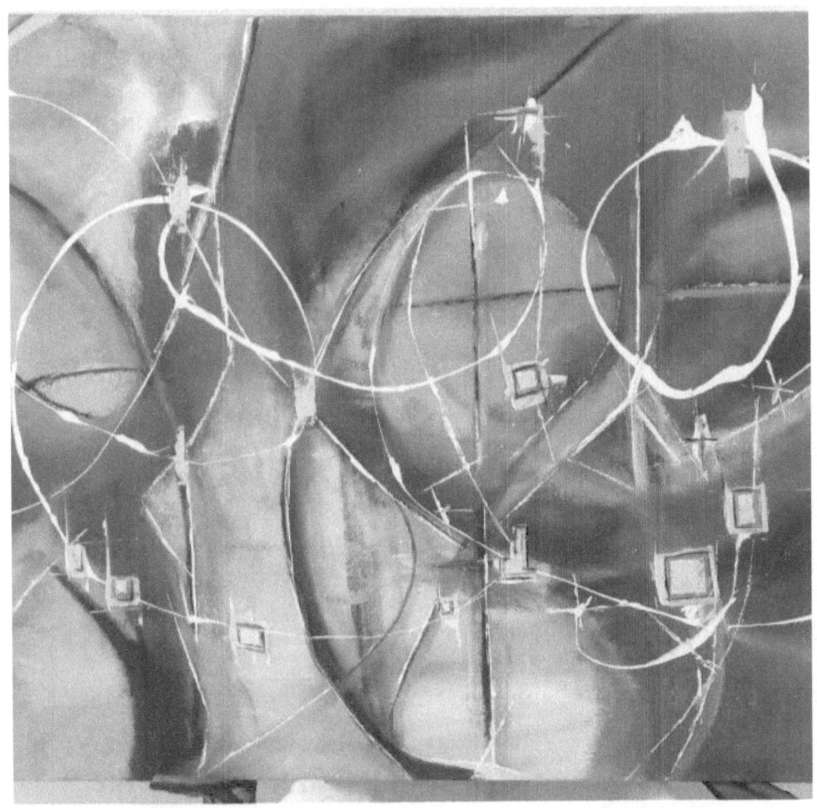

Who is a Freelance Consultant?

So, who is a freelance consultant? A freelance consultant is anyone who has the skills they can leverage to provide business advice and expertise on a contractual basis. These consultants are brought in by private companies to solve problems related to profitability, improve processes, train staff in specific skills and design interventions in the private sector. In the case of the public sector, they are brought in to design economic and social development projects, evaluate projects, implement projects, provide implementation support with expert knowledge and experience and set up processes for innovative development models, usually to enable the poor to get out of poverty or to improve agricultural and dairy production, and further sustainable development. They are more prevalent in the following industries: Construction, architectural practices, legal, certification experts, cosmetics and beauty, health and well-being, and food and nutrition.

The freelance consultant is a problem solver, a negotiator, a planner and an executor. They look at things with a fresh set of eyes. These experts bring solutions to the table which have measurable positive results, which is their value proposition.

There are different types of freelance consultants. The following are the common types:

Business Consultant – One who provides professional services and advice to companies to solve critical problems related to the business such as profitability and helps them achieve their business goals. They improve or optimize processes, improve employee performance through improved training, develop improved business plans, and help improve customer satisfaction.

Financial Consultant – These consultants provide financial advice to companies. They usually work in the private sector with the CFO to support audit preparation, mergers and acquisitions transition, valuation of the company, corporate restructuring, working capital management, and raising IPOs. In the public sector, they aid government procurement processes, monitor project budgets, and support internal and external project audits and reimbursement management with donors. They have good knowledge of financial management, accounting and corporate governance.

Strategy Consultants – They are usually top-notch consultants, also called C-suite consultants. They support private and public-sector companies to achieve long-term business goals. They support business model transformation, and develop organizational strategy, digital strategy and economic policy.

Human Resource Consultant – Small and medium enterprise companies usually do not have an in-house HR Team. They hire human resource consultants for recruitment, induction, succession planning, compensation structuring, change and conflict management, HR policy and documentation development.

Marketing Consultants – These consultants review existing marketing strategies and undertake studies and examine data to see what works and what doesn't. With a new understanding of data analytics, they develop better strategies, giving the company a higher return on investments. Thereafter, they support the rolling out of the new marketing strategy by developing implementation planning, monitoring the execution process and measuring the results of the new strategy.

IT Consultants – Information Technology is now indispensable in both the private and public sectors. IT Consultants help companies choose the right technology and develop the IT infrastructure so that it adds value to the company's profitability and improves work processes. In the public sector, it supports the development of the MIS for projects and programmes. IT consultants work with the in-house IT team and with the MIS manager in setting up the IT system, which includes both software and hardware. They add value to the project through their expertise. There is niche expertise such as cybersecurity and spec-ops, which were earlier used by a hand full of companies, but nowadays it is gaining momentum and popularity and more companies are opting for such expertise.

Management Consultant – A management consultant is one who works with companies in improving processes, solving problems and improving performance.

Value Chain Consultant – These are experts that support the problems and provide solutions to a specific product value chain by analyzing the constraints, when the product moves through a path from production to various agents, till it reaches the final consumer.

Agribusiness Consultant – An Agribusiness consultant works mostly with public sector projects related to agricultural production. They help set up business models for farmers and provide support in improving business processes so that the products can be sold in the market and move across the value chain where the farmers and other stakeholders make profits.

Trade and Market Development Consultant – These consultants support the identification of export and import markets with a higher value for products and identify trading constraints such as tariffs for goods and services. In addition, they are also experts in identifying and valuing domestic markets for various agricultural and industrial products. Their focus is to improve business processes so that the producers get a higher return on investments.

Agricultural Economist - They focus on policy issues and undertake policy analysis of price incentives for farmers and undertake agriculture public expenditure reviews to improve the allocation of resources in the agricultural sector. They undertake an economic analysis of a project or programme and develop a detailed cost table for it. They also evaluate projects and usually work with bilateral and multilateral donor organizations, either through a contractor or by direct recruitment.

Food Systems Development Consultants – They are usually agricultural production experts and nutritionists. They provide solutions to both government and public-sector projects in terms of looking at the entire food system holistically so that sustainable, nutritious food production is possible.

Project Management Consultants – These consultants focus on project scheduling and capacity building of the project team to enable completion of the project within the scheduled time and stipulated cost. They work closely with the project management teams to ensure that the project activities and tasks are organized well and aligned with the corresponding costs so that the project is completed on time. In addition, they undertake the necessary risk analysis and develop control systems before the project is executed. They are usually certified by the Project Management Institute, USA, or by the British or European Commission. They are highly sought after in the private sector and are popularly used in the aeronautical industry, pharma industry and infrastructure companies, to name just a few.

Agriculture Production Consultant – These consultants work in the agricultural sector, focusing on crop production, both food and cash crops. They are expert horticulturalists or agronomists. They help assess the soil, landscape and the production system and support the optimization of resources used so that the farm remains profitable. They advise on seed rate, spacing, nursery management, plant nutrient use, organic farming practices and organic certification. Their emphasis is on the overall productivity of the farm and sustainability of yield in an integrated production system, or a monoculture system.

Livestock Consultants – These consultants work with both the private and public sectors and focus on the well-being of animals and their productivity. They work with bovines, ducks, and poultry. They provide expert service on farm management, improving production, and productivity in the production of milk, meat and eggs. They are experts in managing animal and livestock health.

Fishery Consultants – There are two types of fishery consultants. There are those who work in artisanal fisheries on the high seas and assess fish stocks and ensure sustainable production and the fishing of different species of fish. Meanwhile, the inland experts focus on freshwater fisheries to support production, productivity and fish health management and sustainability.

Health and Well-being Adviser – These experts advise on human fitness and well-being. They work with clinics and fitness clubs and provide specialized services to clients in terms of controlling obesity and managing chronic diseases such as hypertension and diabetes. A few of these consultants have specialized knowledge about nutrition for adults and children and provide nutrition advice.

Image Consultants – Image has become a very important factor in peoples' lives these days. It is supposed to make you feel good and is a crucial part of your existence and is vital to your professional marketability. This is a growing profession, and these professionals are highly in demand in urban areas and in the corporate world. They emphasize on personal grooming and managing your wardrobe.

Life Coach – These freelance consultants focus on human health and well-being. They are trained to support people to 'navigate' difficult periods of their lives. These coaches are certified by the International Coaching Federation, and the National Board for Health and Wellness Coaching.

Freelance consulting is the most fascinating and fulfilling job in the world. It gives you freedom, helps you to develop professionally in subjects and topics of your choice, allows you the opportunity to meet people from various walks of life, visit beautiful and exotic places, build strong relationships and earn money to live within your means. However, there are challenges one faces, especially if you are without a brand, or without the backing of a professional firm. Freelance consultants in the public sector face a different set of challenges when they are from the South. There is a big difference in job opportunities depending on your nationality.

I still like the independence of an independent freelance consultant. This book is all about becoming a freelance consultant where you don't have a brand projecting you, but you are nevertheless the brand you project through your excellent work by using your exceptional knowledge and superior skillset!

In the summer of 2004, I was taking a walk one evening in the town where I lived 20 years ago and came across our local politician. Without a greeting, the first thing he said was that he always wondered what I did for a living. At that time, after having completed my contracted project, I was unemployed and looking for work. This is always the case with most consultants; we prefer to take this time to reflect, relax and plan new coordinates for future work. I really enjoy my downtime because it allows me to spend time with family and friends. So, I told him that I was a consultant and currently preparing for my next assignment. He was surprised and asked me how many clients I had sold insurance to.

"Sorry, I don't sell insurance, and I am not a financial adviser. I am a freelance consultant, and I am not looking for a job. Let's just say I am doing some business," I answered.

"Oh, so now you are interested in business. That's a good move for you to remain unemployed for half the year," he said sarcastically. He wished me luck and walked away with his gang of sycophants.

Time passed by and I managed to get some consulting work from a regional financial institution, which had the mandate of servicing a province bordering China. It was all exciting work; I designed a project for this organization and was paid a good fee. It involved a bit of travelling, which I enjoyed very much. I travelled to a town along the China border and visited a Buddhist monastery. The beauty of the Himalayas was breathtaking and the chants from the monastery still linger in my mind to this today.

One year passed by, and I met the same politician again at a wedding. He was very happy to see me. He asked me again what exactly I did for a living.

"Are you a lecturer? Someone told me that you are teaching, or training at an institute?"

"No, I'm not. Remember I mentioned to you last year that I'm a consultant," I said.

"Do you have a card?" he asked.

 I gave him my card.

"Have you written a book?" he asked.

"No, I haven't."

"Well, how will we know that you are an expert," he said.

At that time, I thought that if I attempted to write a book I would look like an academic. How wrong I was. Little did I know at that time that writing a book would allow me to help many consultants trying to make a living as freelancers.

I picked up my Kindle and searched for a book that would guide me to write a book; I came across *You Must Write a Book* by Honoree Corder. Her book inspired me to write my first book. Towards the end of the book, she wrote the following piece so eloquently, and this became my primordial motivation to write this book:

"You have great things inside of you, and writing is the opportunity to get them out, share them with the world, help make the world a better place in some small way, and be creative at the same time."

As I write this book, there are so many consultants, content writers, business coaches, life coaches and behavioural experts who are building their brands using LinkedIn, Facebook and Instagram as platforms. Many of them are writing blogs and books to enhance their brand as experts, coaches, gurus and consultants. I realize that building a brand may take some time and it is an ongoing process. It takes patience and perseverance to become a life coach, or a nutritionist, an expert consultant in AI and so forth. Of course, there are many who have written spectacular books, which have become overnight bestsellers and they are now consultants or coaches in their craft.

This book is meant for men and women who want to become consultants, particularly for those, who after some work experience, want to become independent freelancers in their own trade. The book provides a set of tools to build your skills and competency to thrive in the competitive world of consultancy.

Can a freelance consultant gain the necessary knowledge and skills, generate business and make a decent living? Knowledge and skills are not enough; there is a lot more you need to be a successful consultant. Branding is a good thing, but it is building relationships with clients and team members from past assignments that will make you most sought after and in high demand. It also has much to do with being at the right place at the right time; meeting the right person at a networking event may provide opportunities for getting interesting work in the future.

With the development of science and technology, there is a great need for improved knowledge and skills, but there is an even greater need for support and service to improve human productivity, happiness and well-being. There is an overload of information on the Internet on productivity, much of which is a repetition of the same best productivity tips. If you spend a few hours watching YouTube videos on productivity, you pretty much know how to be productive.

Organizations need an outsider to look at their work with fresh eyes; they need help in implementing a business strategy or are looking for solutions that will solve their most difficult problems. I knew I had something to share with the world that would help the facilitators and experts do their work better. In this book, I share my experience as a consultant without a brand. My purpose is to provide some insight and share my experience as an independent freelance consultant with a wider range of people in both consulting and non-consulting professions. I do not claim to know everything, and I am sure my mentors and colleagues will have so much more to contribute. This is my version of the skills, knowledge and attitude required to succeed in this business.

Although this book can be read by all professionals, consultants and life coaches, it will resonate well with and be most useful to freelance consultants and individuals working independently. Although these consultants may not be working for a company with a big name, they have developed their personal brand in the sector through their work.

This book is also for those who are working for, or are going to work for large consulting firms or small boutique firms. It is also meant for young graduates who are going to work in a private sector company and those who are going to undertake work with their respective government. It is intended to be a guide for those who are planning to leave a regular day job to become a consultant in any field. Finally, this book is meant for all men and women who are in private or public sector consulting, NGOs and the government.

Consultants without a brand are working in various sectors of the economy, and they have certain specific characteristics that distinguish them from those who work for big brands or boutique firms. They are usually independent, specialized experts, well organized, skilled, smart, creative, and friendly, with a high level of EQ. It is easy to go on about the talents they possess. I have come across a number of these professionals in the different countries where I have worked . When I was completing school, I became a fan of consultants like Ram Charan, and experts like Roberts Chambers.

These are people who have an independent mind, who came out of business school and decided to become consultants by joining a consulting firm during campus recruitment or have trained themselves to become consultants and then joined a reputed firm. There are others who have retired from their job gaining a lot of experience in a specific field of expertise and decided to work as consultants. Then you have those who were pushed out of their jobs due to workplace politics, or those who quit their jobs because of a toxic work environment and had no choice but to become a consultant.

This book will give you all the tips and strategies to help you build the entrepreneurial skills and knowledge to be a successful freelance consultant. The issues discussed and the guidance provided in this book will help you create demand for your services in the consultancy market and maintain long-term relationships with clients and colleagues.

Freelance consulting is an art, and it is possible to prepare your canvas and complete your painting – i.e., learn how to plan your work and life as an independent consultant. Understand what to avoid and what to embrace to be more competent and productive. Learn the skill sets required for consulting and develop them over the years. In addition, this book addresses the concept and principles of rapid skill development and action, the application of skills and testing skills, and how to develop consciousness to learn and sharpen your skills. It covers the strategies to hone your skills as fast as possible. You will learn the techniques to look for work. Last but not least, learn from lessons of the past through a process of regular reflection, and use all your experiences in your next assignment to improve your work.

I will discuss ways to organize your knowledge, which is essentially your bread and butter, that will give you the desired confidence in your field of expertise. You will learn how to become an expert in a subject within weeks. This book not only shows you how to organize knowledge, but also gives you the tools to improve your domain knowledge, focus on key knowledge areas that will improve your consulting practice, look for the right resources, focus on the integration of knowledge, and harvest knowledge for any consulting assignment.

Furthermore, the book focuses on matters that are more than just knowing the tools and techniques in your field of expertise that will make you unique and set you apart, provided of course that you apply what you have learned. You will learn ways to observe while in a consulting assignment, maintain your composure under stress, communicate strategically, ask the right questions, develop the art of going deep in a conversation with your client, and capture insights and build hypotheses. Furthermore, I will show you a success framework that is simple and applicable.

Networking is useful, but I will make you understand how useless it is without a conscious plan and goal. I will show you how to break down your needs and information before joining a networking event so that you are not exploited or disillusioned by someone's behaviour while you are networking. You will also learn how to outline a relationship-building strategy, based on which you can develop one that best suits you. I will also discuss how you can make your presence felt in a networking event.

Since consultants work independently, it becomes imperative that they plan their life. The book addresses what you need to know, when to act, and when to ask for help. It also gives you a framework to plan your year for work and personal goals. You will learn how to plan your week and day. It discusses what habits play a role in the effective planning and execution of your plans.

Values are often undermined in consulting practices. I attempt to define common values, why they are important in consulting, and how they guide individual and group decision-making. In addition, I will discuss value-driven behaviour in dealing with clients and working in teams. I will also discuss what value you can bring to the table when you participate in a consulting assignment and how you can optimize your contribution to the project.

Teams are the vehicles that deliver solutions to clients. An independent consultant becomes a part of a team. These are usually multicultural and multigenerational teams, and one must work in teams for months on end, or for a brief period, say two weeks. You are never working alone. You are either working with a consulting team or a team on the client side. Some teams are unique in terms of their composition and structure while others have a common structure and composition. It is important for a freelance consultant to know how a team is formed, the type of members in the team, how to work in a team and when and why they need to exit the team. Auditing your work after a mission or an assignment and reviewing your conduct with the team is essential to improve your skill sets and knowledge. There are a few tips for navigating a team environment, which will give you rich dividends in the long run.

Reflection is an important part of human nature; we do it consciously and unconsciously. One needs to know why reflection is important in becoming a great consultant. My attempt here is to provide an understanding of how to use the outcomes of reflection to improve your performance in the next assignment and highlight the many ways we don't like to acknowledge our weaknesses, both in our work and behaviour. Lack of this self-knowledge could lead to major disasters in a team activity or compromise the quality of your work in the next assignment. We can reward ourselves and positively reinforce good behaviour and habits during our assignments.

We often ignore the best practices and are inclined to reinvent the wheel. The need to avoid worst practices is more important. I want to reinforce the idea that embracing the best practices and being aware of the worst practices in consulting is a good thing. It helps reduce stress and improves your relationship with team members. For example, critiquing the work of your team members is a professional exercise, and receiving the critique in good spirits is a best practice while bitching about your colleague who has critiqued your work is a worst practice. Your legacy as you become successful and grow in your profession will haunt you, trust me!

Your success framework is something that you will have to develop with hard work and discipline. When I say success framework, I mean the areas that an independent consultant needs to focus on, to be a good professional, husband/partner, father, mother, and friend. It will allow you to have a rewarding life, relishing freedom, happiness, good health and good relationships with your near and dear ones, including your mentors, mentees and colleagues.

Reading habits are crucial in consulting and the ability to surf the net smoothly to pick knowledge areas that are most relevant to your work is important. This helps you keep abreast with today's fast-developing world. LinkedIn trawl is good and if you can do it effectively, you can pick up leads to upcoming work and connect with experts in your field and similar fields. Consulting is not for the faint-hearted and physically weak. It is demanding in terms of your physical and mental energy. You must be fit before, during and after an assignment. You will need to eat well, sleep well and exercise or meditate, which means you must have some discipline to be optimally productive. Family time is crucial for your mental and physical well-being, and in consulting work, you can easily get this wrong. Consulting is a way of life, an art, and is not merely a job.

Chapter 3

Becoming One

There are several ways of becoming a freelance consultant, but the three major ways are as follows: Straight after school, after gaining some work experience, or after losing a regular job.

Straight after school

Some of the top graduate schools of business across the world facilitate placements for consulting firms to choose their employees. Many young men and women join companies like McKinsey, Bain, Deloitte, and BCG. Many professional firms recruit straight out of business school. This system is followed across the world.

Many freelance consultants have started their consulting business on their own, straight out of business school, creative arts and architectural school, engineering institutes, or from vocational training institutes specializing in trades such as electrical, mechanical, sanitation, information technology engineering, finance and insurance, etc. Several of my colleagues and independent consultants that I have worked with started their careers as a consultant straight after school. This phenomenon was more prevalent in Europe, but nowadays, it is becoming common in Asia, Africa and the Americas. Usually, they train themselves in natural sciences, economics, environment, vocational tradecraft and computer science and then work independently in their specialized field.

The current trend is to start blogging their expertise, becoming a YouTuber, demonstrating their knowledge and then advertising on social media platforms like LinkedIn, Instagram and Facebook, leading you to their landing page on their website where they offer online services, training and coaching.

Earlier, when social media was not prevalent, graduates would join as consultants in bilateral and multilateral agencies or local management firms. Most of them, as I found out later, become permanent employees of these organizations, but there are others who continued independently and undertook assignments from different organizations.

If you want to become a freelance consultant straight after graduate school and run a consulting business, then you need to follow a systematic process.

First, you must select one niche area of expertise. You should ask yourself what you want to do and what subject excites you most, where you can use your knowledge and skills to help organizations solve their problems and build their capabilities. Once you have identified this, you should identify your weaknesses and strengths in this field. This is a crucial step because you will have to know everything, both theoretically and practically, about this knowledge domain.

Second, identify the other experts in the field you'd like to pursue as a consultant. Where are these people? What is their background? Where do they work and who are their clients? And to what extent is the area of expertise in demand by the private and public sectors?

Third, you will have to market yourself and at the same time find work. It is extremely difficult to find work as a freelance consultant and it is even more difficult to do so when you are completely new, straight out of graduate school without any experience. It would be to your advantage to prepare a plan to market your skills and solicit clients while simultaneously working on the core skills that you are trying to sell. I will discuss this aspect later in the book in detail.

As a beginner, straight out of graduate school, you must carefully select just one field of expertise and focus on this one thing as you will be working in the world of super specialization.

After some work experience

In 2001, I was working on a UN project, and there I met a United Nations diplomat who was one of the conceptualizers of the project. He usually visited his hometown once a year. When he visited, he would often sneak out of the house to smoke a cigarette in our office, because his wife had banned him from smoking inside the house. During one of those chats, where we discussed life and work, he told us that our project work was like that of an artist who loves his work and with every stroke of his brush on the canvas, he completes a beautiful picture.

His words still echo in the recesses of my mind to date. They are profound, and even today, when I work on any project no matter how difficult it is, I consider it to be my canvas of work and every presentation, every meeting, every field visit and every report becomes a stroke on that canvas. Recently, I came across a book that ricocheted the same thing, but in a more elaborate way. The author, Marcus Buckingham, talks about how we need to see love in our work so that we love what we do for the rest of our life.

To become a good freelance consultant, some work experience is an advantage. This work experience gives you an insider's view of several things when you work with clients. You will be able to use this art on a canvas concept very well as a consultant if you do have work experience.

Men and women work very hard in school and are hired by companies and consulting firms. They learn, build relationships, sharpen their skills and grow their knowledge, but after a while, they feel lost and quit their job to become a freelancer, a YouTuber, blogger, skills trainer or life-skills coach. Somehow, in my view, they have fallen out of love with what they liked doing and have discovered something else to do. I doubt whether they will stick to their second vocation for life. After leaving their first job, many of them aggressively market themselves on social media to sell their skills and become independent coaches and consultants.

After losing a job

After being pushed out of a job fairly or unfairly, freelancing becomes a means for survival. These are guys who think and believe that life is not a dead end. They have put in almost a decade of hard work in an organization and then one day, they find themselves cornered in a toxic whirlpool where they are drowning and must come out of it to survive. These men and women possess specialized and superior knowledge and skills related to a specific topic in the respective industry they work.

Most of these people are either victims of racism or are considered cultural misfits and so forth. However, there are many who failed to move up the ladder and thus removed themselves from the competition. But this group of people have one thing in common: They love what they do. If they didn't, they would never become high-paying consultants. They are confident in their areas of specialization and consider themselves winners. This attitude motivates them and gives them the courage to work with old colleagues, finding their way to becoming professionals with independence and freedom, while simultaneously building relationships with different industries and organizations, creating value for what they do.

Identify which group you fall into. I am sure you will have a lot to say regarding your decision to leave your regular job to become a coach or consultant, or if you're still in school, why you chose to become a freelancer.

- You could discuss the Terms of Reference with a mentor if you have one, or a colleague or team member, to clear any doubts.

During the assignment, you will get to work in teams as well as individually, and you will do the following:

- Read the Terms of Reference of the other team members and identify areas where there is potential overlap of work, and tasks that are dependent on your tasks, or vice versa.
- Usually, a smart team leader would have done this exercise on your behalf and would also expect you to collaborate with your colleagues to discuss and plan these tasks jointly.
- You will have to work more closely with colleagues, have separate meetings and understand how and when they are going to conduct those tasks that are related to your tasks. This collaboration is important to ensure the timely submission of your piece or report and to maintain deadlines.
- This is an opportunity to observe how team members analyze and make decisions, using various analytical techniques, and how they communicate with the team and the client. You will learn several techniques and skills that will be useful for you to develop and learn. You will learn how to improve your communication skills, especially, how to listen actively, pitch a point, make a summary, and provide a conclusion or a recommendation.

During an assignment

What really happens during an assignment varies from assignment to assignment. Usually, you start off with a meeting with the client team, followed by a field visit to factories, banks and other stakeholder offices. You will meet different people and groups of people, as you interview and collect data and documents. Thereafter, you will return home and work on all the data and information you have collected before analyzing and writing a report.

During the assignment, you will learn the following:

- How to interact with people, meaning how you will ask questions that will help you get the right data or information you are looking for.
- You will learn how to pitch issues that you are interested in and get the stakeholders' response. This is an important skill, and it takes a lot of practice. You need to plan your fieldwork, or the interview you intend to conduct, listen carefully, observe the body language and behaviour of the people you are interacting with, and look for the right time to pitch the issue.
- Preparing mentally for surprises is another thing you will have to do so that you learn the art of reacting positively to surprises. There are many surprises that might disappoint you if you are not prepared.
- Note-taking and organizing your thoughts during the assignment is an important skill you will develop. Organizing your thoughts, asking the right questions and then taking accurate notes is important because you may not get the opportunity to do so again. You will have to prepare your notes in a manner such that when you are back at your workspace, you will be able to refresh your memory while preparing the data analysis and analytical narrative in your report.

After an assignment

A lot of the learning and skill-building happens after the assignment, provided the following habits are built:

Reflecting after an assignment will help you to consolidate what you have learned before and during the assignment. This will further help you to hone your skills. What do you reflect on? This is the most crucial question. You should reflect on your behaviour and mental process. What behaviours and mental processes worked before and during the assignment and what didn't work?

Analyze – Analyzing your performance by yourself, with the help of peers and your manager or team leader – quite like a 360-degree evaluation – is a great learning opportunity. You can analyze your behaviour, communication, presentation and analytical skills. In addition, you can analyze what you contributed to the entire assignment and the value you brought to the table. This analysis will lead to the identification of three important aspects that will help you to sharpen your consulting skills:

a. **Discover your weaknesses** and strengths – Discovering your weakness and then converting them to your strengths is an important process of development and progression to become a sound professional. Discovering your strengths will give you confidence for future assignments and is a feel-good factor in the current assignment.

b. **Identify skill gaps** – Identifying skill gaps during the process of analysis will help you cover these gaps in the future through a new learning plan.

c. **Identify knowledge gaps** – Assessing your knowledge gap is very important as a consultant. As you generate knowledge you are also generating important information. As you do that, you will find that there are topics where you are lacking in knowledge. You will also find that there are areas of knowledge where you have some half-baked vague ideas but lack thorough understanding. Then, there are times you feel like you know everything, but you are not confident. Have you ever felt like this? You surely would have if you reflect and think about your work more deeply.

When you feel like this, you have identified gaps in your knowledge. These are your gaps, and you can quickly fill these gaps by undertaking short courses on LinkedIn, Udemy, Skill Nation or Data Camp to name just a few. For example, if you want to brush up on your Excel formulas and shortcuts you could take a course in Excel. Or if you don't have a thorough understanding of export regulation, policies and global value chains, then you might like to brush up on this subject through research documents and studies and supplement your learnings by reading a book written by an expert on global value chains. However, you need to be careful when you are selecting a course. The Internet is littered with courses of all kinds. You must be able to select the right course, with high ratings and from certified instructors.

Plan to develop yourself as a freelance consultant

There are no fixed guidelines for developing yourself as a freelance consultant. However, careful planning for self-development is not an option. It is a dynamic plan that will change after the completion of every assignment.

Mentors are people who will guide you during or after your assignment and will provide honest feedback, acting as a sounding board for ideas and issues. You will have the liberty to discuss critical personal and professional issues with them. They will selflessly support you to move forward in your life as a consultant.

I was once in Africa on a long-term technical assistance project, and there I had a mentor who had also been my team leader in missions in Indonesia. Whenever he thought it was time to have a meeting and discuss work and life, he would tell me, "Hey, I have a nice chunk of meat I bought from the valley which is marinating in my fridge. Would you like to come over for supper?" I would turn up with a bottle of red wine and the mentoring would begin. Those were times when I learned a lot from him about work and life.

It is however difficult to find mentors. Usually, you might find them in your own family, whether it may be within the country or abroad. I believe that those who don't know much about your culture will treat you with respect and will judge you at face value. These mentors will provide you with the best feedback about your personal and professional conduct and guide you in improving professionally.

Books are my best friends, and they should be yours too! There was this lady who had lost everything in her life, I mean her husband, her children and a large portion of her life. She told me that now she had no friends and even I was not her friend anymore because I lived overseas, and we never got to meet and chat. She told me that books were her best friends and when she has no one to talk to she reads a novel. Life to her revolved around eating, reading and living. This example is a bit extreme; however, you must read and make books your friends.

To become a consultant par excellence, you must read voraciously. Reading professional books, articles and other books will help you open your mind and make you more confident. Freelance consultants are at the top of their game. You have no choice but to make reading a habit and a passion.

Becoming a Freelance Consultant is a Journey

Becoming a consultant is a journey. It is a learning process. There are several questions you will have to ask yourself before you take this journey and after embarking on it.

Where do I want to go?

This is the most crucial question. This means, where do you see yourself at the end of the next three or five years? Most often, we set goals honestly, but we don't look at life's time horizons so that we can successfully do what we want to do in our lifetime. We read numerous books on vision and goal setting. We work on it for some time and then another wave of life's hassles overwhelms us and we forget about all the effort we put in after two or three years and quit halfway. Are you a quitter?

When you initially start as a consultant you will be overwhelmed with work, and you must put in the effort to find time to reflect. Reflect on how you conducted the assignment, and how you behaved with your clients, colleagues and stakeholders.

For example, I found myself having numerous bosses for many things and always reflected on whether I made them happy with my delivery and performance. You could be doing work-related reflection, but you may not have the time to set life goals and reflect on life itself. We are caught up in this frenzy to boost our performance at work and be more productive with each passing day. This is all good if it contributes to the milestones you have set in life i.e., your vision or dream to become someone.

So, stop focusing all the time on your professional horizon; allocate time to focus on your personal horizon. So, let's STOP and reflect on what you expect out of life in the next five years. You might find that you need a house of your own, need to find a life partner, need to save for your old age, need to have children and so forth. Or your goal may be to get richer by x% and have a certain bank balance, be a better listener, be a good parent, take care of your parents, or be a leader in your profession or community. You might like to be more charitable or own one of Elon Musk's Tesla cars. There are endless possibilities you can think of.

So clearly, there are two streams of reflection. First, you reflect on your work to improve performance and productivity for future career growth. This is intrinsically tied to the reflection on your achievements and where you would like to be in the next five to eight years. Second, you reflect on your personal and life goals. This is about developing yourself to become a good human being, physically fit, meditative, patient, calm, overcoming your addictions to alcohol, smoking, social media, etc., and having a healthy with relationships with friends, parents, siblings, your spouse and children.

What are my weaknesses?

Our weaknesses are very difficult to understand, identify and detect; in contrast, it is much easier to detect weaknesses in others. As a consultant, dealing with your weaknesses on a day-to-day basis will be your greatest challenge and a learning exercise for self-improvement.

Questioning yourself on your weakness needs to be a systematic exercise. There are three core weaknesses:

The most important weakness is that pertaining to your health – because of the stresses in modern life, you could have chronic weaknesses and diseases such as hypertension, diabetes, irritable bowel syndrome (IBS), poor eyesight and weak limbs.

Secondly, you may have weaknesses in dealing with difficult situations and having conversations on technical matters with colleagues and your family regarding work. These weaknesses are mainly psychological, related to your personality type and your energy management. They usually affect your communication style, tone and pitch, which are reflected in both your verbal, non-verbal (body language) and written communication. Often, these weaknesses show up when dealing with colleagues and clients while on a project.

Thirdly, you may be weak in your skills - you don't have certain skills required in your field of expertise and this impacts your confidence level. These weaknesses show up while you are analyzing a situation, identifying and finding a solution to a problem. They emerge when you compare your abilities with that of your work colleagues.

It is good to analyze your weaknesses. We will discuss how to overcome these weaknesses in the following chapters.

What are my strengths?

Identifying your strengths is much easier than identifying your weaknesses. You are keenly aware of what you are good at. For example, you are good at something, and everyone wants to compete with you in this skill, but you come out on top. You have skills that are rare, and you know this. So, it's easier to identify your strengths rather than your weakness. However, in consulting you cannot sit on your laurels and hope for the best. You must fine-tune your strengths; use your strengths in more flexible and creative ways.

There are three ways of finding your strengths, which are cardinal to being a good consultant:

First is your *strength of character* - This is your ability to be ethical, honest and forthright. Your ability to say 'No' when needed. Your ability to draw boundaries to ensure that you are safe from both psychological, social and physical harm. This strength is very important if you are to be respected in the consulting business. Even the ex-CEO of one of the big consulting firms didn't work on strengthening his character and found himself in trouble and in jail.

Working on your character will help you avoid plagiarizing, copying and mimicking others. This will make you and your work authentic. Your colleagues, clients and seniors will respect you. This strength will take you a long way as an independent consultant.

The second is *mental and physical strength* – The mind is elastic, and it can be strengthened like the muscles of your body. To be a good consultant you will have to be mentally and physically strong. Many consultants take this lightly and as a result face burnout.

You will need to test yourself to measure this strength. You need to ask yourself how long you can stand and listen to a conversation with full concentration; how much can you write without error with the minimum amount of sleep; how long can you sit in one meeting, expanding your attention span for more than ten minutes. How long can you walk on the farm and climb hills to see the source of water for a rural water project? These are strengths that you need to find out.

You are often in good shape mentally when you are in good shape physically. A regular schedule of exercise and meditation and at least seven hours of uninterrupted sleep is required to be mentally and physically ready for a consulting assignment. When you need to stand for long hours listening to conversations to ascertain qualitative data, when you need to walk for long stretches in the sun while visiting a village, or climb hills, or when you sit in meetings with stakeholders while you are bombarded with data, information and reports, you must be in good shape to perform well.

Third is your strength *of information, knowledge and skills* – This set of strengths will allow you to thrive in your business, making you a good player in the game. Ask yourself how good you are at collecting information to get a good understanding of the project before you take a decision or propose a solution to your client. How much domain knowledge do you have? Are you able to keep up with the growing body of knowledge in your domain area? Do you have adequate analytical skills using Excel, STATA, SPSS, R or Python? How good are your skills in preparing a storyline/storyboard in a PowerPoint presentation?

Once you have the answers to these questions you will either forget about it or consciously prepare a plan to improve your strength in being well-informed, knowledgeable and skilled. This will depend on how you have trained yourself in becoming a consultant. This is what this book is all about!

Mind map your pathway to becoming a consultant

There are several pathways to becoming a good consultant and independently working and running your consultancy business. You need to figure out which pathway to take. Mind mapping is a useful tool to be able to figure out how you will work your way up to the top. The mapping exercise will help you recognize the many pathways for the various skills, knowledge areas and networking that you need to identify and learn. According to Tony Buzman, "A mind map is the ultimate organizational thinking tool. And it is so simple." I would recommend his book, *How to Mind Map* to help you develop this skill.

If your central idea is related to becoming an independent consultant, then the branches emanating from the central idea will increase your knowledge, skills, and contracts with clients.

General Capabilities Required in Freelancing

There are numerous general capabilities required to be a freelance consultant working in a firm or independently in various industries. They include the following: Developing domain knowledge, ability to work at a certain speed, data and information synthesis, good memory, high level of quantitative skills, observation skills, listening skills, communication and presentation skills, and computer skills.

Domain knowledge – A consultant is an expert in his area and domain knowledge. Domain knowledge is not static, it is dynamic. All domain areas are growing with the development of research and knowledge management. You must proactively assess how much domain knowledge you have in your field of expertise. These improvements in domain knowledge will happen when you learn from your recent work, read research material, and books, hold conversations with your mentors, undertake short courses or a combination of all these strategies. You must be on top of things to give the best solution and advice to your client.

Ability to work with speed – Speed is the key to demonstrating that you are an expert and providing value for the time spent on the assignment. If you are working for a contractor like McKinsey, Bane, BCG, EY or Deloitte, you will be expected to work at top speed. If you are working for UN projects where consulting missions last for 12-to-22-day sprints, you will be expected to work at top speed. This means gathering data and information, analyzing and coming up with an analytical narrative, conclusions and recommendations. This must be in sync with the kind of input provided by the team members and must satisfy the team leader or manager responsible for the mission or assignment.

Data and Information Synthesis Capabilities

Digital Skills – In consulting, everything that you tell a client must be based on evidence in the form of data and information collected by you firsthand. Even if it is from a secondary data source, it must contribute to hard evidence. Hence, the ability to not only collect data but to collate and analyze the data and synthesis this information to lead to conclusions and recommendations is a critical capability of a consultant.

Good Memory – A good memory is a blessing! After I completed my PhD, I decided to work as a manager in a private company with a big brand name. I started out as a lateral recruit without a business degree and here I am with two MBAs from a premier business school in Asia. I was awe-struck by how two of my work colleagues could memorize numbers, from remembering the basic price to the MRPs of various products, including the names and telephone numbers of dealers and retailers. It was mind-blowing and they were simply impressive. I almost had an inferiority complex. I told myself that I would need to build my memory by undertaking memory-building exercises or putting in extra effort to improve my memory. I cannot underscore enough the need for a good memory.

Quantitative Skills – Clients want everything that you say, the logic that you give, the analysis that you make, the conclusions that you draw and the recommendations that you make backed by numbers. So, to have high quantitative skills you must have the ability to use numbers to make sense of a situation by analyzing the numbers using arithmetic or statistics.

Most consultants are highly skilled in statistics, econometrics and financial mathematics. They are generally good with numbers. This is a must if you want to be top-notch. They are not only skilled in the theoretical aspects but also in the practical application of statistics and mathematics. They are extremely skilled in the use of MS Excel, SPSS, STATA and R software. Engineers are experts in the use of quantitative survey software and design software like CAD, Bin Software Engineering Studio and other architectural design tools.

Observation Skills – This is a skill that is often ignored. You can get much of your information and insights from observational data.

In the winter of 2002, I was travelling with a new team leader from UNOPS, who had recently been handed over the project, on which I was working, for supervision. He was a calm person with a Chinese mother and a Punjabi father, the eldest son. He had done his MBA from a British university. Let us call him the Hybrid Monk for the sake of this discussion.

Hybrid Monk asked me, "Do you observe everything around you?" while passing through a crowded, bustling city.

"Yes, I do observe everything around me," I answered.

"What do you see?"

"I see a lot of chaos, noise and dirt around me."

"That is the exact reflection of the mind of the people in this city – chaotic, full of noise, and dust."

I was shocked! According to the Hybrid Monk, the minds of the people living in the city were dirty, chaotic and noisy. When I think about this conversation, I feel it says a lot about observational data and the conclusions one draws from such data. Hybrid Monk told me about many interesting things over the course of two and a half years, which I shall address in the later chapters.

Observation is not that simple. You can observe a phenomenon, a person, group behaviour or the landscape around you. This must be done in a systematic manner. You must decide what you want to note from your observation that would provide data for the case or the problem you are trying to support. For example, observing human behaviour in a factory will tell you a lot about the quality of production, rate of production, and motivation of the workers in doing what they are doing. As a consultant, you cannot miss data that comes from close and careful observation, or *intentional observation*.

Listening Skills – This is another very important skill. I remember a situation when I joined a private sector company as a manager. We were invited to a meeting where all the new recruits were invited by the Chairman of the company to a gathering where he was going to formally welcome us to the company. We entered the room. The Chairman was already sitting at the head of the table and the VP was next to him. The Chairman asked each one of us to speak a little about ourselves. We all did. The VP spoke, asked a few questions and welcomed us. All along, the Chairman just listened intently. He didn't interrupt and remained calm all throughout. I wondered whether he was really interested in what we had to say. I was quite perplexed. A few months later, I was again at the head office with another colleague. The Chairman bumped into him, called him by his first name and asked whether his sister had completed her final exam which she was supposed to have finished a few months after our induction.

As a consultant, you must listen actively. You must not only understand the words but the meaning behind the words, the tone and the emotions. You must be fully attentive to be able to capture the key issues, understand the situation, identify the problem and provide a solution. Today, the cell phone in your pocket is the most distractive object and obstructs effective listening. Next, is the pen you hold to scribble anything and everything. When did you last see a colleague doodling in an important client meeting as if to say that the topic being discussed was not part of his/her Terms of Reference? In consulting, paying attention to details, paying attention to clients and listening actively to them are ways of showing respect.

Communication and presentation skills – Both verbal and written communication is key to becoming a successful consultant. It is even more important if you are working for a larger brand or the Big Five because clients have higher expectations.

Making a presentation to a client in a conference hall or auditorium is the same in terms of tension and nervousness. Stage fright is real and to be a good consultant you must be able to prepare professional slide decks and simultaneously give a convincing presentation to your clients. Most good consultants have good presentation skills and can communicate with an audience with ease. But this is not easy; it takes a lot of practice.

Recently, I was listening to a video podcast of Dr. Gopika Kumar, an author and a soft skills specialist from New Delhi, India. She was speaking about how to become a great communicator, public speaker and presenter using the acronym STAGE, which I will try to explain the way I understand it. I would recommend that you read her book *Personal Power Equation: Step by Step Blue Print to Magnify Your Image – The Ultimate Book on Personality Development, Communications and Soft Skills Enhancement.*

According to Dr. Kumar, when it comes to public speaking and presentation skills, the S stands for a simple entree sentence; T stands for technical aspects to pay attention to at a granular level, so much so that you even decide on the type and size of the mike to be used, the size of the stage, its height, the venue, etc.; A stands for active engagement, which means gaining proximity with the audience and asking the audience to undertake an activity to shift the attention to the audience; G stands for gestures – using hand gestures and body language for open communication to sustain the attention of the audience; E stands for eye contact, where she recommends initial contact should be made at the top of the head and later with more confidence look at the eye level of the audience, especially when you cannot see the audience. She underscores how important it is to build self-confidence in public speaking.

So, public speaking and verbal communication is the key. However, doing a professional presentation is not easy. You need to learn to use the PowerPoint app to make professional slides. There are numerous courses on PowerPoint presentations offered by Skills Nation and other former consultants from big management consulting companies. There are several techniques to develop good charts and one should look at the 'Chart of the Week' available on the McKinsey app. I would recommend that you take a course in developing PowerPoint presentations provided by management consultants on Udemy, or YouTube.

Consultants must have strong public speaking skills. However, most shy away from training themselves. They carry their fear on to the stage, in front of a large or small audience. The biggest fear of a freelance consultant is that of public speaking.

Dale Carnegie mentioned in his book *Public Speaking for Success – The Complete Programme* that most people taking public speaking courses want to conquer their nervousness. He talks about the essentials of public speaking, which I believe are also important for freelance consultants:

"Start with a strong and persistent desire. Know thoroughly what you are going to talk about."

Computer skills – To be a top-tier freelance consultant requires a very high level of computer skills. You must have the ability to use statistical software and programming languages based on the type of industry you are serving. A minimum requirement would be the ability to use MS Excel skillfully. Even if you are a nutrition consultant, a well-being coach or a freelance makeup artist, you need to know how to use MS Word, PowerPoint and MS Excel. You may need to write a programme for a client, an official letter, give a presentation of your products, or keep accounts. You should be able to program in Excel, use most of the shortcut keys and be proficient in creating tables and graphs, especially if you are a regular freelance management consultant or an economic or social development freelance consultant.

You should be able to use special statistical packages such as SPSS, STATA and R, especially if you are in the fields of marketing, data science, or economic development. You should be able to program in Python if you are working in a more sophisticated engineering field. Of course, you don't need to be good at everything that I have mentioned above, but depending on the industry you are working in, you will have to build such computer skills. If you are an IT consultant, then data science, data management, digital transformation, building interactive websites, developing apps, algorithms and AI are some of the areas that you will need to build your skills. The most pressing need for freelancers across any field today is to develop the skills to utilize Chat GTP for their work. You must be familiar with and an expert in programming languages, and web development languages, although the future of this is quite grim with the development of Chat GTP 4 where the AI software can program in almost all the programming languages that have been updated and fed into the system.

Looking for Work

It is a shameless endeavour! You literally must be shameless and ask for work. This is the reality. Most positions that you may have qualified for in the UN system are taken away through nepotism and connections. Regarding the top jobs in multilateral organizations, they are taken by graduates from the elite Ivy League group of universities, or from sandstone universities in the UK or Europe. If you are from an Asian, African or Latin American University, your chances of getting a job in these institutions are slim. Moreover, these organizations are heavily funded by the West, and they want their youth at the helm of affairs. Well, that is quite fair. They make the rules, and you follow them. Recently, private consulting companies have stepped into this space, providing better opportunities for freelance consultants. Don't misread my intention in writing this; I don't feel bad about the whole thing, I'm just stating the facts!

There are several strategies that you can adopt to get consulting assignments. These are briefly outlined below and will help you develop your own strategy for acquiring work.

Applying to consulting companies – Many young graduates from prominent business schools are picked up by consulting companies during campus recruitment programmes and job fairs. If you want to join a consulting company as an independent expert, you must apply for vacancies that they have already advertised on their website or send in your CV to be included in their consultant's dossier. But this will not lead you to your first job. This is only to make your presence felt.

Applying to both multilateral and bilateral organizations – The same way you apply for a job at consulting companies you can apply to bilateral and multilateral organizations. You must continuously visit their website for vacancies and projects. This is a game of luck and chance. These organizations will be keen to hire you as a consultant when they have a good reference from other consultants or project managers you have worked with or perhaps one of your professors for whom you have done some work in the past. For example, unless you are from an Ivy League university, where the alumnus has created a good impression and demonstrated the skills that the HR team of that specific organization you have applied to is looking for, it is most likely that another Ivy League graduate will be spotted before you during the application process. This background check is the required criteria only for regular jobs in such organizations. You don't have to be from these institutions to be a freelance consultant. What you need is the skillsets and experience to work for multilateral and bilateral organizations pertaining to the areas of expertise that they require.

Using DevNet – This is a website that is dedicated to advertising jobs in the development sector including long and short-term consultancy assignments. This website is often used by most development agencies. These include multilateral, bilateral, private companies, and NGOs. You can apply for jobs on this website, but it must be a part of your multi-pronged approach. If you don't know anyone or don't have a good reference, or you are not from one of Europe's elite institutions, you will not make it. Sounds a bit negative, right? But this is the reality. You must build a strong network to be able to get a good long-term or short-term assignment.

Let me tell you what I mean by a multi-pronged approach when it comes to looking for consultancy work. Consultants are often selected based on where they come from, meaning the geographical location, citizenship, religion, the university attended, and mindset – whether it's Western or conservative, or fundamental belief system, like do you burn incense sticks in your office? God help you if you do, as I was judged to be religious for burning incense sticks in a stinking office room in India. Even inconsequential things like whether you have a beard or not, or whether you are vegetarian or not, matter. Your connections and your referee, if you have one, also matter. So, when you apply for a job or a short-term contract on DevNet Jobs, do not stop there. Find out if you know anyone currently working in the organization, or anyone who has worked in the organization in the past. Look for a good reference!

Writing to colleagues – It is important to keep in touch with colleagues whom you have worked with before no matter how short a duration it might have been. It should be a part of your relationship and networking efforts. Networking is something I will talk about a little later in the book. Your old colleagues might be able to inform you about assignments in the future or give you a reference for an assignment if the contractors are keen to know more about you and your work or competency.

Writing to friends – Friends are our greatest source of information whom we usually underestimate and undervalue. This is because we consider friendship to be a tool for our relaxation and often engage in personal discussions that are purely for entertainment. We may have friends in the same industry who could be useful in providing information or introduce us to someone who could give us consulting work. They might also broaden our knowledge of difficult problems and issues the industry is dealing with.

Using social media resources for job hunting – This is another important source of information to get consulting work. It is, therefore, important to develop a very clear and accurate profile of yourself and your work on LinkedIn. This will help recruiters using LinkedIn to easily spot your talent and expertise. I was hired by Ernst & Young thanks to my LinkedIn profile, although it is not very impressive; I need to work on it myself.

Websites – This is another strategy to look for work. Every organization has a website these days. This includes large multinationals, small and medium enterprises, and government organizations. First, before you even apply for work, you need to go through their websites to understand the kind of business they are in and the activities they are undertaking. Does it match your area of expertise? Second, look for departments and their leaders, and the contact information of the decision-makers. This will help you connect with them for queries regarding work. You could send in your CV or write a letter to HR informing them about your work experience and the value you would add if they hired you as a freelancer to solve their organizational and business problems.

Consulting firms – Consulting firms are today the largest employers of independent consultants. We have Ernst & Young, Bain, BCG, McKinsey and many other boutique consulting firms that hire freelance consultants through LinkedIn and from CVs already in their dossier.

Write to recruiters – Over the last decade, several global recruiters have mushroomed in the hiring landscape. Linda Arneis for example, recruits experts and specialists for development agencies and projects. There are several recruiters like Ms Kakar and her organization in New Delhi. There are many recruiters looking to hire experts through ads on LinkedIn and other marketing channels.

Summary

You can become a freelance consultant straight after school or after some work experience. At both levels, you will need the knowledge and skills to become an effective and successful consultant.

While trying to become a freelance consultant, you need to focus on building skills and learning during the process. It is important to build a learning mindset.

You will have to learn before, during and after an assignment.

There are no perfect guidelines available to develop yourself. You must plan your own development to become a good consultant.

You must take the support of mentors, read books, and journals and attend training courses to develop yourself.

The biggest exercise is to understand yourself, to understand your weaknesses and strengths. Then, work on your weaknesses and capitalize on your strengths.

Reskilling is a very important activity you will need to do to be able to provide the best service to your client. Reskilling is initiated in large public and private sectors and even large consulting companies. Many of these skills include analytical skills, social skills, security skills and communication skills. Skills to build and retain clients is important, in addition to your deep domain knowledge and technology skills. Companies use algorithms to identify the skills required for their staff and develop reskilling programmes.

Build communication skills, computer skills, domain skills, technology skills and digital skills so that you are ready to work in any environment. You need to discover the type of skill that is required for you to survive and be the best in your domain of expertise. You might have high-demand knowledge but might lack other skills, such as communication and digital skills. Young consultants, in future, will have to be able to develop skills to interphase with AI to provide value-added services to their clients.

Chapter 4

Growing Your Skills Tree

One can build skills in completely new areas, or in the old areas of expertise. You will have the highest level of skills in an area where you love to build your expertise and the passion to continue building them. But often, we are not able to do so because we don't put in the time required to practice our craft to be the best in the world.

Most often, you can't be what you want to be because you don't do what you really want to do. These are the vocations suitable for us where perhaps we can naturally build our desired skills. I wanted to be an artist, but the best I could do was to exhibit my work in Eswatini, Africa, where a friend of mine from Belgium was kind enough to organize an exhibition for me. Thereafter, I stopped pursuing this path, because I was busy with my economic consulting assignment. I still haven't figured out till today what had stopped me from doing what I had to do to become an expert, or what withheld me from building advanced skills in consulting like learning Python programming. It seemed at that time as if an undesired force had prevented me from doing what I had to do. Perhaps, if I had pursued my passion for painting, I could have become very good at the craft that is so dear to my heart. It is very easy to build new skills and sharpen old skills when it comes to something that you are passionate about and is close to your heart.

This undesired force is defined by Steven Press Field in his book *The War of Art – Break Through the Blocks and Win Your Inner Creative Battle* as Resistance. He writes, "Resistance cannot be seen, touched, heard, or smelled. But it can be felt. We experience it as an energy field radiating from a work-in-potential. It's a repelling force. It's negative. Its aim is to shove us away, distract us, prevent us from doing our work."

Freelance consultants need to build skills consistently because we are pros and not amateurs and we fight resistance every day. We work late into the night to complete a report or wake up early to complete an analysis and send it to our colleague to compile it as a part of a report. We do what must be done without making a fuss about it. To fight the resistance to sit at a hotel desk, or at a Starbucks Cafe and complete your work is a skill that you must hone by fighting negativity, fatigue, boredom, anxiety, and any other form of resistance.

The Importance of Skills in Consulting

Honing your skills as fast as possible is critical to becoming a freelance consultant. You need to develop a variety of skills, including the use of analytical software, preparing professional slide decks for presentations, taking notes, preparing analysis for presenting info-graphs, writing professional reports, and soft skills like handling a client, listening to his needs and perspectives, managing your team members and colleagues and the project manager.

You will need excellent skills in using MS Excel, MS PowerPoint, and other presentation software such as Think Cell, programming software like R, STATA and languages such as Python, Html, PHP, Java and other variants, etc.

Hence, the skills that you need are the following:

Computer skills – These skills fall under two categories: The first is using presentation, word processing and statistical software, while the second set of skills involves computer programming in different languages. In both public and private sector consulting, you will need to develop skills in programming languages, programming in Excel, STATA and R. Learning how to program in Python, especially if you are a freelance data scientist and other languages, and being familiar with different statistical techniques is a must. Skills in data science, which is a super-specialized field of expertise, are also critical. In construction management and civil engineering, you might have to learn how to use Bin Studio and CAD. This list could go on. The moot point here is you must become a super expert in using the software that is relevant to your field of expertise, developing a digital mindset.

Paul Leonardi and Tsedal Neeley in their book *The Digital Mindset - What It Really Takes to Thrive in the Age of Data, Algorithms, and AI, define* a digital mind this way: *"It is the set of approaches we use to make sense of, and make use of, data and technology. The set of attitudes and behaviours that enable people and organizations to see new possibilities and chart a path for the future."* They further mention that digital forces such as big data, AI, robotic teammates and internal social media, blockchain, experimentation, statistics, security and rapid change are disrupting the way we interact with our colleagues and clients.

They propose that the way to approach the digital mindset is through three fundamental processes: Collaboration, Computation and Change. They explain that the redefinition of the approach through these processes means one needs to learn and develop new skills and then use these new skills to see the big picture and ask important questions. Developing a new mindset means that one must develop new skills and see the world in a new way and change their behaviour r accordingly.

Communications skills – The art of observing, listening and talking. We need to communicate with colleagues, stakeholders and clients. Honing your communications skills involves the ability to mentally organize your thoughts before clearly communicating with an individual, or group and ensuring that they understand what you are communicating. There are various communication formats. These include face-to-face communication, real or virtual, email communication, telephonic and virtual or direct presentation.

Having all these skills will contribute in the following ways:

- Your collaboration with colleagues will be enhanced
- Speed of delivery will improve
- Quality of work will be better
- Clients will be more satisfied with your advice
- Time management will be better

Planning for Skill Development

Skill development will require a plan. The steps to developing the plan are given below:

Identify the skills that you already have. This self-review of skills is very important to build confidence and know yourself better. List the skills that you already have and check which ones are relevant to your domain of interest and what has become obsolete. For example, you were good at programming using Basic and Fortran, but today you need to be good at Python, C++ and Java and so forth. Soon, these will become obsolete with the evolution of Chat GTP. Are you good at any of these? Do you have basic knowledge, or do you have to learn from scratch? Do you have to become skilled in Machine Learning, and AI?

You must prepare a plan to improve your existing skills and learn new ones. Then, prepare a timetable for learning and developing these skills within a year or two.

Identify new skills that you need to learn to do your job. If you are already in a job at a consulting firm, you will notice that you are good at certain things when you compare yourself with your colleagues. You will also notice that you are not as good at many other things, such as developing a financial model within an evening to be presented to your team leader or client. You may not be as fast as your colleague in building a deck of slides in record time. If this is the case, then you need to figure out how these colleagues do what they do so well. Speak to them and learn from them. Give up your ego and work with them and learn. You need to be humble enough to learn and develop these skills by lending a hand or asking them to teach you.

Identify the available training programmes online. In addition to learning from your colleagues, find out if there are any online resources to help improve your skills. The web has a vast number of resources for you to pick and choose. You may come across an excellent training course offered by a retired or freelance consultant. Take the course to develop your skill! This is a good investment in yourself.

Undertake the training course and commit to completing it.

Very few people complete an online training course once they have enrolled. Just about 20% of people complete a training course. So, in a sense, offline courses in a classroom environment are more effective in terms of completion of the course. To take an online training course you need to be very sure if you need the course and how it will benefit you. To get the best out of an online training course, do the following:

- Be sure to identify the area of expertise you need before you choose the training course.
- List the best training companies like Allison, Udemy, Coursera and other institutes and universities you know that offer the type of course you are looking for.
- See the course rating given by other trainees.
- Check the cost of the training and make a tradeoff between quality and cost.
- Most importantly, check the duration of the course.
- Check how many other courses you have enrolled in and whether you have completed them. Please complete the previous courses before undertaking a new course.

- Next, you need to schedule time on your calendar to undertake this course.
- As a matter of best practice, you should dedicate a time slot every day to the online course that you have enrolled in.

Rapid Skills Development and Action

For those of you who want to start a career in consulting regardless of the kind of training you have had in the past, regardless of whether you are in public or private sector consulting, there are numerous skills you need to hone as quickly as possible. The main skills developed during your school years are not enough for freelancing.

- Structuring your thoughts and actions.
- Building competency in communication skills.
- Team building skills.
- Building IT skills.
- Building social media skills.
- Planning skills.
- Building social skills and being aware of business etiquette.

Structuring Your Thoughts and Actions

During a consulting assignment, you will be bombarded with a lot of data and information from discussions, interviews, reports and field observations. Next, you will need to analyze the data and information and come up with ideas, informed views, notes, solutions, reports and recommendations. It is immensely important to organize your thoughts before you organize the data and information and mentally prepare a summary of your analysis. This will help you to further act on the data and information based on what you are expected to do next. It could mean that you need to prepare a report, summarize your findings in a meeting or influence a client or stakeholder.

Barbara Minto in her book *The Pyramid Principles – Logic in Writing and Thinking,* illustrates how the mind sorts information into groups, forming a pyramid. The thoughts and ideas are then broken down into lower groups. This is a structured way of communication, stating the ideas first and then putting together the supporting evidence. According to Minto, it helps busy executives to absorb messages quickly because of the vertical relationships between the key points.

The pyramid comprises the top level, which is a summary of the key points, followed below by the second level of key points supporting the first level, and then the third level with data and information supporting the second level.

Liz Kenney, an ex-McKinsey consultant from My Consulting Offer, states: "The Pyramid Principle is a valuable communication tool that you can use for case interviews or any time you want to make a persuasive argument." According to her, the core elements of the Pyramid Principle for communication are the following:

"**Lead with the answer first.** The most important part of the Pyramid Principle is to make your recommendation(s) right away.

Support the answer with key facts and insights at a high level. Synthesize the main takeaways from your analysis that support or even challenge your recommendations.

Back key insights up with detailed data, analysis, and evidence. These backup pages will probably include many of the analyses you perform first and summaries of the evidence you gather. These data points help you and your listener understand the situation clearly and see how it all adds up to your recommendations."

When you use the pyramid principle for written or verbal communication, you are using a structured way of first answering the question straight away, then supporting your answers with facts and insights, and eventually backing the facts and insights with data, analysis and evidence. Furthermore, you can use the same method to structure your actions following top-down logic and reasoning.

There are four logical ways of structuring your ideas which are given below in the illustration:

Deductively – which entails a major premise, minor premise and conclusion.

Chronologically – which is structured as first, second, third, and so on.

Structurally – in terms of City 1, City 2, City 3, and so on, relating to spatial structure.

Comparatively – the first most important point, second most important point, third important point, and so on.

IDEA LOGIC

Four Logical ways in which to order a set of ideas

Deductively	• Major premise • Minor premise • Conclusion
Chronologically	• First • Second • Third
Structurally	• East Dalrich • Mbabane • Hoho
Comparatively	• First most important • Second most important • Third most important

Let me now show you an illustration pertaining to the structuring of a message/idea for writing and communication in a presentation or when having a discussion with clients. It involves two logical sequences: Vertical **logic** and **horizontal logic.**

The next diagram illustrates the vertical logical structure of the presentation for a hypothetical project to purchase a TATA trucks franchise for the Estwani Truck Market in Southern Africa.

Again, here's another example of using the vertical logical structure by asking the 'how' question sequentially as you progress in your verbal and written communication.

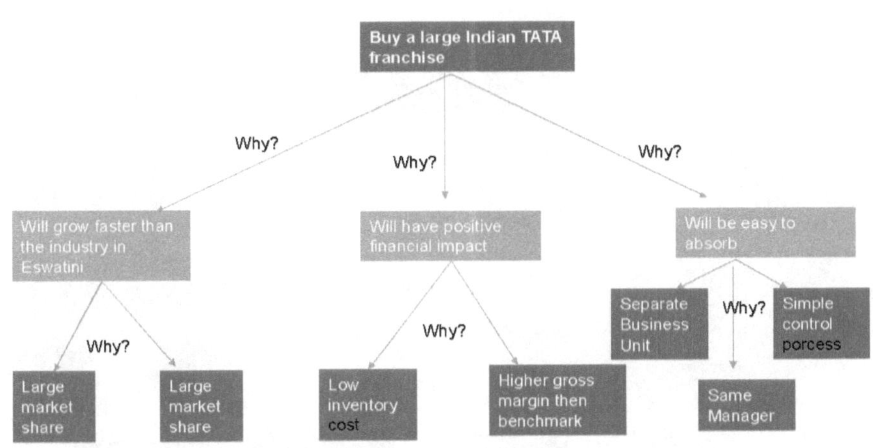

Structure showing using "How" is used structuring in steps

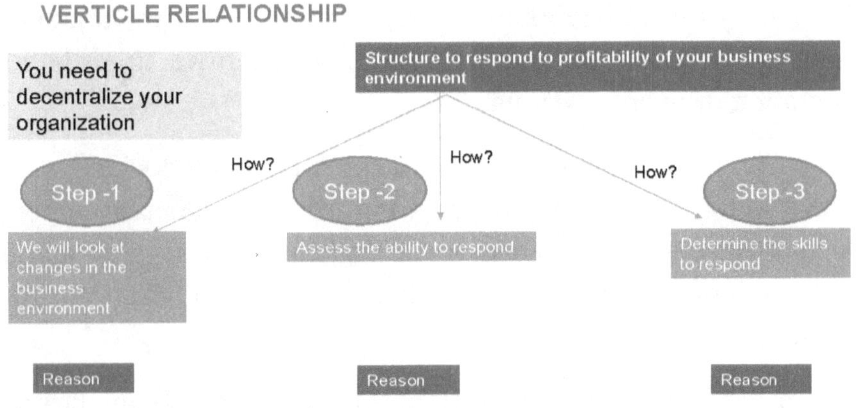

The next is an example of developing a structure for both written and verbal communication using a step-by-step sequence, giving 'reason' and asking the 'how' question.

Shows the use of step by step structuring using 'How?" with reasons

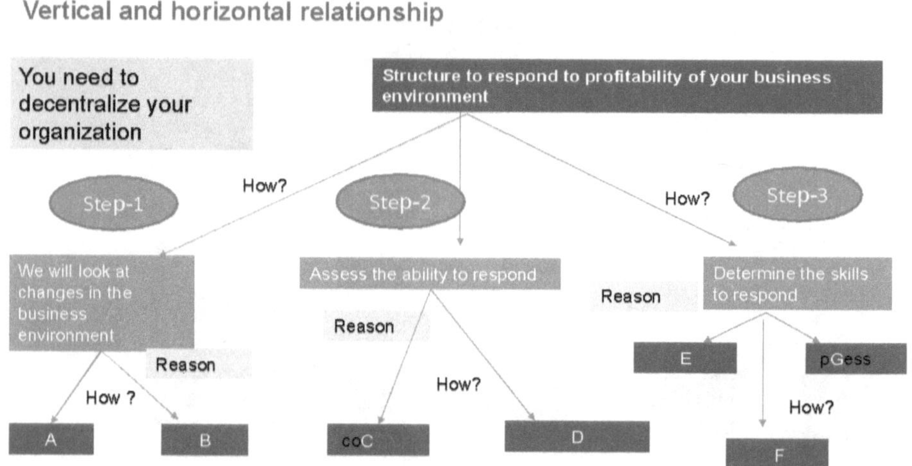

Structured thinking helps you frame your thinking in a manner that your thinking and analysis are logical, helping you clearly express what you intend to express without confusing anyone. This framework also ensures that your arguments are coherent and precise without faltering on logic or narration. It also helps you to be repetitive either in your presentation or in your writing.

Storyboarding is a common structured thinking method which is used for developing a convincing presentation, which is persuasive enough to encourage your clients to decide and act based on your presentation. This is an effective presentation that a consultant gives during a consulting mission.

The framework can help to address issues, constraints and complications that must be addressed to arrive at a solution to a specific problem or to achieve a set of desired results or outcomes.

Building Competency with Different Types of Communication Skills

Learning how to communicate early in your career, starting from the time you are in school is important. However, it is never too late to learn. You can do this by first being aware of the way you communicate. Take an online training course on communications skills, the use of social media, professional writing and storytelling. Read books on communication, especially those that focus on writing effective emails, and body language. Here are some tips that will help you communicate effectively as an independent consultant:

Face-to-face communication –

- In face-to-face communication, take care to maintain eye contact in a non-threatening manner. Your head movement, sound and tone of your voice need to be mild and non-threatening. It should make the other person or group feel comfortable, and they should perceive that you are listening, and interested in what they have to say.

- Showing interest in what the person with whom you are having a face-to-face interaction with has to say is vital for you to be appreciated and your message to be heard. Your body language should be open and non-threatening. You need to ensure that you keep a formal posture while communicating in business. This is challenging when using Skype or MS Teams, where your facial expression and the tone of your voice matters the most. There is very little room for body language.

- When you start a consulting assignment, as a thumb rule, you should listen 80% and speak (pose questions) 20% of the time. This is very important to understand so that you will be accepted by your client. No matter how experienced you are, and how well you know the issues and the solutions to resolve them, you should never speak your mind in the first few meetings; just listen to what the clients have to say. You will be surprised to find how much you don't know and how wrong you are.

Telephonic communication

Telephonic communication is one of the most difficult forms of communication to create an impact as you don't see the person you are talking to, especially if you have never met physically or on MS Teams or Skype. However, this might be the best opportunity to create a good impression and connect for work.

In 1992, I was working as an assistant professor at a state university, and I had to speak to a management development coach from Coverdale, a development management consulting company based in London. I was very excited and spoke fast, hoping to get the information through to her. The coach listened for a while and the first thing she asked me was my name. Addressing me by my first name, she started speaking very slowly, one word at a time. The next sentences I uttered were automatically at her pace, which was spontaneous. This was a remarkable experience – how one person whom I had never met could influence me to speak slowly from almost 11,000 miles away in another country. I still remember this experience. Hence, she demonstrated the power of communicating over the telephone. What I learned from this experience are the following:

- You must prepare mentally what you plan to discuss over the telephone.
- Be brief, and later you can elaborate on the topic in an email.
- Make sure to ask for the person's name and address her by her first name.
- Find a quiet place to take a call and if you receive a call on a train, bus, or aircraft, tell the caller you will call later.

- Always take a call from a quiet place, a quiet office, a quiet corner of a hallway or a quiet corner of a cafe – the noise will force you to increase your pitch and make you speak faster than required, often irritating the person on the other end.
- You need to speak slowly, listen and respond and continue like this.
- Keep the conversation brief. If it entails a lot of complex issues that need more explanation with more data and information, tell the other person that you will elaborate on the issues in an email. You are now just highlighting the main points of concern.
- If you call first, then always mention the purpose of the call. Thereafter, stop and see if the other person has a response. Then, very briefly mention what you have to say, or if you are receiving a call, listen to what the other person has to say. Take a deep breath to control your tone, which should be balanced and neutral; you should speak slowly.
- If you see the conversation is taking longer than expected request another call, or you could tell the other person that you would reply via email with more details and request for his or her email ID if you don't already have it.

Emails

In today's world, email communication is recognized as both a formal and informal mode of communication. Most often, these emails are sent in an unplanned manner and the person receiving the mail is left utterly confused. Likewise, we receive several emails and wonder what they are for.

Felix Haller in his book *Awesome Email – 10 Email Principles to Improve Your Communication and Accelerate Your Careers* mentions the following principle for writing emails:

1. Craft insightful subject lines – Here he mentions that one needs to be specific, appeal to utility, specify actions, and use prefixes.

2. Think of your readers first – He mentions that one needs to aim for a 'yes' response, double check the recipient's name and personalize and compliment your recipient.
3. Clarify expectations.
4. Mention context, message, and actions.
5. Write short emails.
6. Create scannable emails.
7. Use bullet points.
8. Simplify your writing.
9. Leverage email functions.
10. Reply promptly and in line.

(Source: Adopted from www.felixhaller.org)

This is a useful book to read and check out the amazing website. The author, Felix Haller, worked at Bain & Company as a management consultant for six years. He shares his experiences and insights in this book.

Writing a good email is an art and this is an indispensable skill for an independent consultant and those working in management consulting. In my experience, I feel that apart from the use of the above principles illustrated by Mr. Haller, you should try to complete the body of the email within three paragraphs. Anything more than three paragraphs should go as an attachment like a 3 to 10-page note. People are pressed for time and are not interested in reading long emails.

Remember the subject line is the key: It should tell the reader what this email is all about in one sentence; is it information requested or sent, is it about action to be taken on a matter, or is it an invitation for a meeting, seminar, conference, etc. Everything needs to be crystal clear in the subject line.

Language skills

Speaking a foreign language and being able to read and write in the language is indeed a great achievement. In international organizations like the United Nations and in multilateral banks like the World Bank, Asian Development and European Investment Bank and BRIC Bank, you are expected to know any one of these languages aside from English: French, Spanish, Russian, Chinese, and Portuguese.

Many organizations also prefer the knowledge of regional languages such as Dari, Swahili, Urdu, Bahasa Indonesia, Malay and so forth. In public sector consulting, especially if you happen to be working in a country very often, it would be useful to learn the local language. This gives the impression that you are immersed in the culture of the country in which you work as an expat. It helps to build a trust-based relationship with your client and your local staff.

There are several online language courses offered by language experts all over the world. Udemy offers many courses. In addition, many local embassies offer courses. I learned Thai and Russian from local experts. My wife helps me improve my Russian. So, doing business in Russia became a lot easier as I could order a cup of coffee, read a note, understand the outline of a presentation and so on.

Building Computer Skills

Computer skills are required by almost all consultants and lawyers these days. They include:

Speed word processing and editing

As a consultant, you are all the time writing notes, emails, reports and little snippets for larger reports being composed by your colleague where they want your input, on your computer. Very rarely you will be able to produce an output using your computer, may it be an Excel table, a graph or an analytical narrative, in your own time. There will always be a demand in terms of urgency and importance, and you will be expected to deliver something on short notice, or a timeline will be set by someone else. You really need to learn to type fast. You must have a word processing speed of around 70 to 80 words per minute. So, you need to take two important steps:

First, start learning how to type by downloading a typing or word processing software. There are many open-source software available on the Internet. Spend at least an hour daily to practice.

Second, you need to increase your speed. There are many apps that will help you increase your word per minute and test your typing speed and accuracy. Unfortunately, not all universities insist that students learn how to type. I have seen many of my fellow consultants type with their index fingers. In the universities of the South, this is considered a clerical skill, but remember, it is essential to become a seasoned professional.

Speed Reading Skill

In consulting assignments, you will be inundated with notes, presentations, reports and Excel tables. To study all these reports and get a grasp of the context and situation, you need speed reading skills to read all that is provided to you, distil all the relevant information, and reject the information that is not useful. You will always feel guilty if you haven't read a report before meeting the client.

Kam Knight, in his book *Speed Reading – Learn to Read a 200+ Page Book in 1 Hour* writes that 65% of the human brain is used to process visual information. The eyes, as an extension of the brain, contain 2 million components and 12 million photoreceptors to process visual information. He also mentions that experts assert that 90% of the information comes through the eyes. Hence, the human eyes can process text, visual diagrams, sketches, photos, maps and live terrain.

Spreadsheet skills

This is the third skill that a consultant needs to develop. The use of spreadsheet software such as Excel and Google Sheets is important. If you embark on qualitative research in your field of expertise you will need to develop your skills to use software for narrative analysis. You should develop advanced skills to undertake the analysis of data with speed and accuracy.

Speed + Accuracy = Efficiency

Being efficient in handling large volumes of data in spreadsheet format is a much-needed skill in consulting. If you are a data scientist, then this should be part and parcel of your entire skill set. If you have this under your belt, you will be in high demand, considering the contemporary demand in the field of marketing and business analysis.

Data Analytic Skills

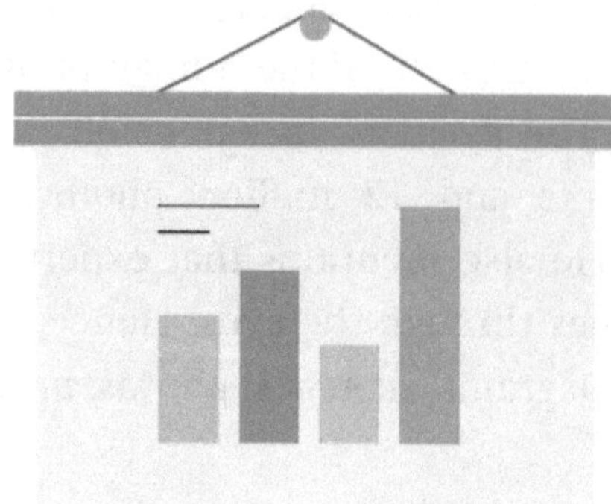

Data analytics is a type of skill that is required by almost all consultants at different levels to undertake a range of analyses in the public and private sectors. You need to choose the techniques that are the most relevant to you. Some of the common analytical techniques used by consultants are the following:

- Simple descriptive analyses such as mean, median, mode with pie charts, histograms, etc. It might include doing different forecasts of data trends.
- Financial data modelling – This entails preparing financial models, a cost-benefit analysis, profit and loss analysis, cash flow analysis, analysis to value a company, etc. These analyses can easily be undertaken in Excel.
- To analyze large data sets, you can use software such as R, SAS and for relatively smaller data sets, you can use SPSS or STATA. Learning how to programme in R or STATA to undertake complex statistical analysis is a skill that takes time to develop. These skills in a consultant are highly in demand.

Presentation Skills

Presentation skills are one of the most important skills for a consultant to hone, whether you work for a firm, or independently. Your keynote presentation, presentation on findings and recommendations, or one that talks about the process to follow to solve the problem must be accurate.

There are many training courses offered on the Internet. There are free YouTube videos and paid online courses that are worth investing in to learn how to prepare professional slides.

Your slide deck must be prepared following these steps:

First, you need to think through and brainstorm what you are going present.

Second, prepare a storyboard and draw a blueprint of the things you are going to present on a single page. This will include slides with a slide action title, a sketch of the graph, subtitles and footnotes.

Third, prepare the slides based on the blueprint and sequence them to tell the story.

Finally, the deck needs to be shared with colleagues for their contribution and comments to fine-tune the deck before the presentation.

Practice giving your presentation before you present it to the clients. I cannot underscore the importance of practising your presentation enough.

Smart websites

There are smart websites which when used judiciously will give you an edge over the others. These are the following:

JOTTI - https://virusscan.jotti.org/

The transfer of a deadly virus into your computer is scary because it can corrupt your original files and the entire computer. As a consultant, you will receive many Word or Excel files and photos via email. Before opening the attachment, use the JOTTI website to scan the file for viruses. You need to go to this website and drop the file to scan for viruses.

PRINT FRIENDLY - https://www.printfriendly.com/

This website can be used to print pages from a website. Usually, when you try to print a page from a website, you find that everything on the page is printed but a large portion of it is not useful material besides the content. You can paste the URL of the website and the specific page you want to print here and delete what you don't need to print. Furthermore, you can even convert the page to a PDF file and print it.

BLUSH - https://blush.design/

In consulting, you need to prepare slide decks and reports. As the saying goes, "A picture speaks more than a thousand words." Pictures and cartoons can be used to convey a message or idea. This website contains many images which you can customize as per your requirement for the purpose of using it in your presentation or reports. You can opt for the pro plan or the figment sketch setup on the website for more professional image creation.

MIXKIT – https://mixkit.co/

This website contains videos, music, templates and icons. There are numerous videos related to an array of topics from lifestyle, nature, men, women, animals, etc., which you can use in your presentations.

Cobot Text Editors

Here's a list of Cobot text editors which you can use to prepare correct summaries of text and notes and to fix typo and grammatical errors:

- UltraEdit
- Microsoft Visual Studio Code
- Sublime Text
- Atom
- Vim
- Bracket
- Notepad++
- Espresso

Building Social Media Skills

Social media is now a powerful tool for personal branding and marketing. You need to know how to use social media, especially to prepare social media blogs to share your experience and views. This tool is sometimes used by different consultants to promote their work and acquire more assignments. You can learn these skills first by taking a training course and then actually creating social media posts. Let me briefly outline how social media can be used to create your *digital footprint*.

LinkedIn

This is a very useful tool for a consultant to build his reputation and brand. This platform tells you the consultant's profile and his latest activities and engagements. With public sector projects, this platform is often used during implementation to share information about successful events, outputs and results of projects in the form of blog posts. I recommend that consultants use this with permission from the team and contractor.

Instagram

Photos and videos of new initiatives and successful conferences and meetings are shared on Instagram. This media is yet to be fully exploited by consultants in their work. Implementation consultants can use this media as a part of a larger scaling plan of best practices to share their high-impact results. This requires a more planned approach wherein the results can be published as a still photo or video. The results in the form of outputs and outcomes can be published in different forms:

- Infrastructure output in still photos
- Seminars, and videos of outcome report presentations
- Progress in the development process as a series of photos or videos
- Videos of policy dialogues and policy development processes
- Product development videos

Facebook

There are various ways to use Facebook. You can use it randomly to post family photos or holiday photos. You can also use it more professionally, posting interesting aspects about your work and assignments with photos and videos. Your friends and colleagues need to know the good things that you are doing.

Consciousness to Learn and Sharpen Your Social Skills

Building social skills and business etiquette

This is an important skill that a consultant must have after developing all the skills that I have already mentioned in the foregone sections. You can make a conscious effort to sharpen your social skills and your etiquette in the business of consulting.

Kara Ronin has a very interesting best-selling course for developing social skills which is called *Business Etiquette 101: Social Skills*. I highly recommend this course to anyone planning a career as a consultant and starting a consulting business. She talks about the elements of 'Know,' 'Like' and 'Trust' as a foundation for developing social skills and business etiquette. She also goes on to teach you how to dress appropriately. I will discuss the dress code for consultants later in the book. In addition, she also covers networking and how to move to the next level, how to start and end a conversation, common conversation tips, and how to build your digital footprint. Her course, which comprises 28 videos, is available on Udemy.

Skill Audit

Knowing oneself well is like discovering gold. As an expert in any field of knowledge, you need to be on top of things, including your skills. For you to grow a new leaf or sprout new buds in your skill tree, you must ask yourself two questions at the end of each year: a) Are my current skills adequate and how much do I need to improve? b) What new skills do I need to learn to remain relevant in my field of expertise?

There are two ways to do this audit: Evaluation of the skills gap with the help of a coach or systematic self-reflection. In both cases, you need to use a pen and paper to list out what skills you have and where you need to improve and what new skills you need to learn. A coach or a mentor can help in this process. I recommend that you use a mentor or coach, especially early in your career. This approach should be combined with self-reflection.

Summary

- As a consultant, you need to grow your skill tree by adding new skills or improving on your old skills. You need to do this as soon as possible without procrastinating so that you are prepared and ready for your next assignment.
- Communication and computer skills are the two most important skills to begin a career in consulting.
- Skill development is a planned initiative – you must identify the skills you already have and the skills that you will need to develop in an assignment and do your job.
- Rapid skill development involves structuring your thoughts and actions, building competency in communication skills, team building skills, IT skills, social media skills, planning skills, social skills and business etiquette.

- You must learn to refine your social skills and business etiquette to succeed as a consultant in the public or private sector.
- Finally, you need to annually audit your skills, so that you know what skills to fine-tune and what new skills you need to develop to remain relevant in your field of expertise.

Growing Your Knowledge Tree

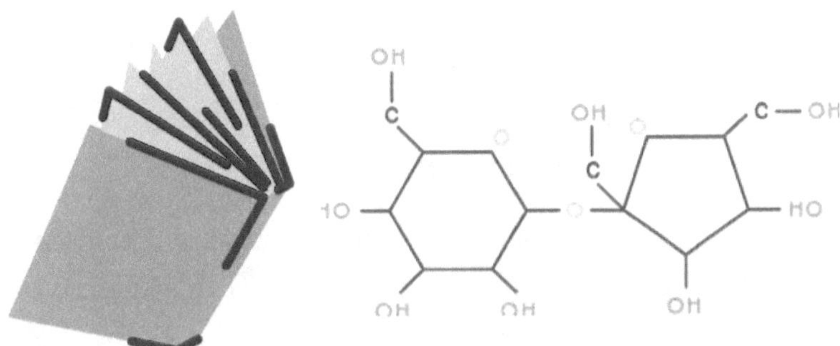

Taiago Forte, in his book *Building a Second Brain – A Proven Method to Organize your Digital Life and Unlock Your Potential*, wrote eloquently: "Instantaneous access to the world's knowledge through the Internet was supposed to educate and inform us, but instead it has created a society-wide poverty of attention."

Life is all about continuous learning, but how we learn and gather knowledge also impacts our quality of thoughts and the quality of life we lead.

How Do You Organize the Knowledge You Need?

You will need to observe, read, ideate and take notes. Note-taking is a habit that all consultants need to cultivate. Many use mind maps, others note down keywords and then later, they articulate and reflect on the keywords, making sense of it all.

You need to write your thoughts down clearly on a notepad. Draw associations between thoughts, points and keywords to have a concrete idea as to what you are thinking and trying to understand.

First, you need to be able to collect data and information and ideas from others and yourself. Second, you need to associate the ideas and information that you have harnessed. Iago Forte writes:

"There are four essential capabilities that we can rely on a Second Brain to perform for us:

1. Making our ideas concrete.
2. Revealing new associations between ideas.
3. Incubating our ideas over time.
4. Sharpening our unique perspectives.

Forte mentions that "Digital notes aren't physical, but they are virtual. They turn vague concepts into tangible entities that can be observed, rearranged, edited, and combined together."

In his book *Building a Second Brain*, he mentions the three stages of knowledge management – Remembering, Connecting and Creating. Forte's book is worth reading to learn how to build your knowledge tree and manage your knowledge by unlocking selected digital devices to create, store and share digital knowledge.

Improve Your Domain Knowledge

Domain knowledge is what makes you a first-stage expert. This is the knowledge by which you are generally hired and offered work early in your career, aside from the fact that you are assessed on whether you have natural learning skills, whether you are a problem solver, can get along with others and whether you can build lasting relationships with others.

To be a domain expert you must first like what you do and enjoy learning new aspects in your field of knowledge domain. This requires a lot of reflection to understand what is relevant and important to you. It is also a combination of knowledge and skills that you must focus on. The crucial part is to develop skills together with the growing knowledge in your field of expertise.

Focus Is the Key

Consultants don't have the luxury of time. There is pressure from both clients and management to deliver the solutions to a problem within a well-defined timeline. Every matter is considered a 'priority' and 'urgent'. Most of you who are already working as consultants, or have worked on consulting projects in the past, understand very well what I am talking about. Hence, the most important skill to build is the ability to focus. The ability to look at any issue or task with 100% attentiveness and have a clear understanding before delivering what is needed to be delivered.

So how do you focus? Focus is a product of mental exercise and the work environment. The mental exercise is as follows:

- First, remove all physical distractions.
- Second, remove all mental distractions; this is something you need to develop early on.
- Third, dwell on the thing that you are supposed to work on by working in time boxes of 15 to 20 minutes, taking a five-minute break and coming back to it.

The above exercise is effective, allowing you to accomplish a lot without much difficulty if you have a peaceful work environment. This environment can be built at your home office, or in your office space at work. However, on the field, you don't have the chance to create a congenial environment, and your work desk at your hotel is the best you can afford.

Sarah Harvey in her book *Kaizen – The Japanese Method for Transforming Habits One Small Step at a Time,* has outlined a way to create your office space to provide a congenial environment for you to work. She mentions that a)You need good lighting, that is white light, for your workspace; b)Surround yourself with photos and postcards that make you feel happy and uplift your mood; c)Place potted plants in your office; d)Surround yourself with good aromas such as aroma oils or things that smell nice; e)Get rid of the clutter by spending around five minutes to clear your office cabinet and work space; f)Make your office storage space look pretty.

The above is only possible in your own home or at work, but not when you are working in your client's office, or in a hotel room. When working from a hotel, ensure that you select a 4-star boutique or luxury hotel where you can request a room with a work desk and a comfortable chair. Many of these hotels already have this furniture. Request for some flowers in the room and some room fragrance and extra bottles of water (to keep yourself hydrated when you work). I normally request for some good seed coffee at least twice a day, while working in the hotel. You need to ensure that you have the hotel Internet code for you to log in to the Internet with your phone and your computer so that your family, colleagues, and clients can reach you whenever they want unless you have informed them of a time slot when you are open to receiving calls and responding to WhatsApp and email messages.

With all the physical distractions removed and the work environment set, it is important to remove mental distractions to focus. This is the difficult bit. The human mind has hundreds of thoughts swarming in the brain. One way to be aware of distractive thoughts is to meditate early in the morning or for a few minutes in the afternoon along with deep breathing exercises. You can find a number of these techniques offered by specialist instructors on YouTube.

So, before you start focusing on your task at hand you need to take a deep breath and understand what is expected of you, and what will be the end result once you have completed the task or activity. Will it give you a better understanding of an issue? Are you to provide any insights, or read, understand and subsequently write a note, or a paragraph or two to contribute to a larger piece of work? Once you have a good understanding of what you need to do to achieve the desired results, you need to stick to the schedule you have set for yourself.

Silence and Quiet to Improve Focus

"Speak only when you feel that your words are better than silence."

– Anonymous

Our ability to focus is often reduced due to distraction. To remain focused, you must be able to work without distraction. Nir Eyal et Al in their book *Indistractble – How to Control Your Attention and Choose Your Life*, writes in the introduction that some products and services are easy to use while others are distracting. The point to note is that distraction can go out of hand, and if you cannot manage distraction, then your mind will be bothered by 'time-wasting diversions.' The authors put it very simply as: Distraction is "action that moves us away from what we really want," and Traction on the other hand is "action that moves us towards what we really want."

Next, you need to learn how to focus by being silent and quiet in a meeting with colleagues and clients when you or someone else is leading the discussion. The art of good listening is important, but even before you start listening to said and unsaid words you need to be quiet and calm. These are the prerequisites for understanding, learning, steering a discussion and coming to a consensus of understanding for action. I have seen experienced consultants, bureaucrats, and technocrats muddle up every meeting and often come out of it with the wrong impression, often stressed and unable to appreciate the takeaways.

Meetings are a small segment of the learning and knowledge-building process. But the ability to maintain calm under duress is important. These difficult situations are when you learn the most as you encounter challenging issues and circumstances. Remaining calm is a skill that you need to develop, to learn and act decisively.

Learning from a situation needs patience, awareness and energy to observe, reflect, act and interact. The ability to learn leads to the enhancement of knowledge which is crucial for a consultant as you wade through the massive amount of information that flows as you move through your assignment.

Jacqueline Brassey et al, in their book *Deliberate Calm – How to Lean and Lead in a Volatile World,* describe the four operating model pillars on page 225 for "Dual Awareness and Deliberate Calm." These pillars are as follows: Your awareness, your purpose, your energy, and your relationships. This personal operating model framework is explained in further detail. I recommend that you read this book published by McKinsey & Company. It provides a model for learning and building your knowledge to be able to manage and lead in times of uncertainty and volatility. It is meant for leaders but is equally useful to freelance consultants, whether you work in the government, or in a corporate ecosystem.

Building Your Own Mental Model for Learning and Knowledge-Building

"When you have to take hard decisions flip a coin. Why? When the coin is in the air, you suddenly know what you are hoping for."

– Anonymous

It is rather daunting to be able to develop a learning and knowledge-building framework or model for yourself. Organizing your thoughts around an issue and thinking deeply is a difficult mental process and organizing your thoughts around several different issues and trying to build a relationship is even more difficult. This requires a lot of practice. So, at some point, you will need to build a mental model to deal with several issues, to learn from the issues and increase your knowledge. This is crucial if you wish to be the best in your profession. Everyone has a unique temperament, interests, capacities and knowledge. Hence, it is important for you to reflect to be the best version of yourself when it comes to learning and developing knowledge. You could try the following steps:

- Take a piece of paper and pen and write down your current behaviour for learning and developing knowledge.
- Sketch out the process you have been following thus far and what impact it has had on improving your learning and knowledge-building efforts.
- How much time do you invest in reading, writing, solving problems, discussing and questioning issues leading to new understanding, information and knowledge?
- Try improving this process to come up with a more solid way of learning and knowledge-building.
- While preparing your new mental framework for learning and building knowledge, ensure that time is an important variable. From my personal experience, time-bound learning on any issue, situation or subject is the best way to learn and develop your knowledge.

Your own mental model will be quite different from the consulting frameworks used by consultants. However, consulting frameworks can help you grow a thought process in understanding a situation, or your client's business problems. You could refer to the following book: *Consulting Frameworks – Use on Your Next Startup, in an Existing Small Business, or to Ace the Case Interview,* by Peter Oliver. This book covers a wide range of frameworks that are used by McKinsey, Bain and BCG.

These frameworks can be used to solve consulting problems mainly in industries and in the private sector. The book discusses the steps in a case interview – identifying the problem, analyzing the problem, formulating options, making decisions, summarizing the case and making recommendations. It is a great book to read. Read it together with *Bulletproof Problem Solving – The One Skill that Changes Everything*, by Charles Conn and Robert McLean. The book goes through the steps involved in solving problems in the real world in great detail and is a must-read for anyone interested in starting a career in consulting.

According to Bernard Garrette, Corey Phelps, and Oliver Sibony, "Problem-solving is a dominant form of how we think and one of our most complex intellectual activities is the core of what makes us human." So, as consultants, we solve problems both quickly and slowly; sometimes we solve small problems and at other times, big problems. In their book *Crack It! – How to Solve Big Problems and Sell Solutions Like Top Strategy Consultants*, the authors focus on solving big problems that affect us or a large population or a region and identify five pitfalls of problem-solving, namely: 1) Flawed Problem Definition; 2) Solution Confirmation; 3) Wrong Framework; 4) Narrow Framing; and 5) Miscommunication.

These five pitfalls are elaborated with case studies, and the book is a great read for consultants involved in strategy consulting. In addition, they explain the three problem-solving pathways: The hypothesis-driven pathway, the issue-driven pathway, and the design-thinking pathway, and thereafter they explain how to solve big problems: Stating the problem, structuring the problem, solving the problem, and selling the solution.

Mental models are more useful when understanding problems and solving problems in public sector projects. A consultant is continuously trying to grasp issues and problems on the field, in the factories or at the client's office. They need to think through the problems and issues. This necessitates the use of mental models. Out of all the mental models proposed by scholars, the First Principle Thinking is the most useful for consultants. This is the same model proposed by billionaire Elon Musk. According to the book, *The Great Mental Models – General Thinking Concepts*, published by Farnam Street Publications, "First Principles Thinking is one of the best ways to reverse-engineer complicated situations and unleash creative possibility." The book states that there are two ways to establish First Principles: a) Socratic questioning and b) The five 'Whys' method.

Socratic thinking proposed in the book leads to six steps (Pg.: 81/82):

1. Clarifying your thinking and explaining the origins of your ideas.
2. Challenging assumptions.
3. Looking for evidence.
4. Considering alternative perspectives.
5. Examining consequences and implications.
6. Questioning the original questions.

The book states that "The goal of the five 'Whys' is to land on a 'What' or 'How.'" This process will eventually lead to separating reliable knowledge from assumptions.

Many years ago, while I was in Nepal on a mission, I met an Indonesian irrigation expert for a multinational bank. Apart from his skills in the casino, he was an excellent communicator. I remember one day while we were discussing work in a restaurant, he told me that at the bank he worked for, he was trained to throw away as many documents, only keeping the ones which were most relevant and necessary for reading and referencing. It not only helped remove clutter, but it facilitated the reading of only what was necessary for a specific assignment.

As a consultant, you will be provided with numerous documents in digital or hard copy format by your clients and colleagues. You will be inundated with documents, notes and reports. The volume can sometimes be enormous, especially when you combine the various documents and reports that you have gathered through the website by yourself. It is important to pick and choose what is most relevant to read, take notes, filing the most critical documents for future use. Dispose of the rest.

Likewise, it is important to know which books you should read. There are best sellers and wonderful books related to different topics of current interest. There are great novels to read. Novels are often read before bedtime, or you could read during a vacation, or while travelling. However, books to build your domain knowledge need to be read rather selectively. For example, if you want to improve your knowledge about blockchain because you are a financial expert, then you need to select books that are related to blockchain and finance. You should ideally not read a book about change management when you are focusing on building your knowledge base on blockchain. So, you must focus! You need to be focused on your learning and knowledge-building effort.

In addition, to select the most relevant books in your knowledge domain, you could pick from the books referenced in a specific book and articles and case studies published in journals related to the theme, or the knowledge domain.

Plan Your Learning and Build Your Knowledge

Learning and building your knowledge tree don't happen by fluke. It is a planned exercise and needs effort and time. First, you need to identify the knowledge you are building your expertise in that you have often recognized through different assignments. This is crucial, because sometimes you might feel that value chain development, marketing and agribusiness are similar, but they are distinct knowledge areas.

For example, marketing can include developing a distribution system, developing distributors and retailer schemes, and brand building through a social media marketing campaign. Value chain expertise includes the knowledge of the value chain itself, margin analysis, upgrading analysis, price incentive and public expenditure support analysis. Over time, you might be able to develop expertise in all three areas, but initially, you should focus on building expertise one at a time.

When you are sitting idle without any assignment on hand, you must plan your learning and knowledge-building. You can take the following steps to plan and execute your plan:

*Step -1: **Select the area you are considered by experts and your employers as an expert**.* This will give you a good assessment of why you are in demand. Here, you need to ask yourself whether you like this area of expertise for which you are always in demand. I hope you do! If you don't, then you are in a bit of trouble. In consulting, you must have a reputation in an area of expertise to get assignments. Transitioning to another area of expertise you are passionate about but where you have little, or no experience, and attempting to get new assignments will be extremely difficult. So, stick to what you are known to be good at by others and not what you think you are good at.

*Step -2: **You must prepare a plan for learning.*** This means that you will have to identify different sources of learning. There are different sources of learning and developing your knowledge areas:

- Read selected books.
- Take a training course to refine and update yourself on the latest in your field of expertise.
- Use the Internet to look for open-source blogs, case studies, and published papers to read.
- Attend online seminars and workshops.
- Connect with your colleagues to find out about new areas to keep up with, or discuss completed assignments and learn from such assignments.
- Explore relevant topics on YouTube.
- Download guidelines and manuals to read.

*Step – 3: **Recording what you have learned**.* This is a crucial part of planned learning. You need to make notes and keep a record of everything that you've learned. You must do the following to record what you have learned, to tap into this knowledge in the future:

- Prepare a notebook or a journal for learning.
- Prepare a file with plastic folders to keep hard copies of reports, published and working papers.
- Buy colour markers and tags to mark books and articles and tag pages and chapters in books.
- Prepare a learning and knowledge folder for each topic to file soft copies of downloaded materials that you have already read.
- Download *Liquid Text onto* your desktop and laptop to download reports, manuals and documents to read, write notes and record and connect important topics and themes. You can subscribe to Liquid Text which is a very useful software for a consultant to have.

While building your knowledge is a continuous activity as a consultant, so is the ability to apply your knowledge to the situation at hand in a consulting assignment. This integration of knowledge in a consulting context is easier said than done. Bear in mind that each consulting situation and context is different, but at the same time, there will be a few common threads of issues and knowledge that will emerge. While observing the events on the field, you will learn about the context over a short period of time, talking to stakeholders and others in formal and informal meetings. Then, you will have the reports provided by the client, your own documentation on the project and Internet search results. It is not any random way that you integrate knowledge. You will have to follow steps to integrate your knowledge with the assignment, which is a planned exercise that you consciously and purposefully undertake.

These are the following steps that I usually undertake before an assignment:

- First, I go through the Terms of Reference of the assignment at least thrice. The first round is a general reading, the second round highlights important components and deliverables of the assignment, and in the third round, I underline and mark the areas relevant to my work directly.

- Once I have had a good idea about what needs to be done in the assignment, I prepare a table with two columns, one to write down what I already know about the components and issues that I have encountered in similar assignments, and the other to write down what I need to know. I leave it for a day and revisit the table the next day to expand it.

Next, I add a few more columns to this table to cover the sources of information – ways to collect more information on the areas where I have little or no knowledge. Usually, I add columns for the source of information, type of interaction, type of documentation and format. Integrating is like revealing new associations between ideas as stated by Forte. When you read the Terms of Reference, you will experience a flow of ideas and issues that you need to look for in the assignment. This is very pronounced, depending on your level of experience. The more experience you have in a particular area of expertise, the more ideas will keep flowing. Now you need to rationalize these ideas and integrate them.

Summary

- Learning and building your knowledge tree to become a better independent consultant cannot be done without identifying what knowledge must be organized for a specific assignment.
- You must develop and build the domain knowledge of your expertise and simultaneously build your skills.
- You must focus and work in time boxes to learn and acquire knowledge. The ability to remove distractions and work systematically is the key. So, you must focus to grow your knowledge tree. Being quiet and calm will help you focus. The more excited you are, the less you will be able to focus and be mentally ready to observe, ask the right questions, learn, harness and retain new information and knowledge.

- Learn how to identify what is not required for learning and what is irrelevant and unimportant. Throw these into the bin and clear your desk from clutter. This will help you to organize your learning. It will help you learn and build knowledge that is relevant and important for you to become an expert in your field.

- The ability to organize your thoughts during a consulting assignment is an important skill. Each one of us, based on our ability, temperament, memory and patience, must develop our own framework and a mental model to learn and increase our knowledge, which we can dip into to develop solutions and provide recommendations for our clients. You can also use standard consulting frameworks used by consulting firms.

- Plan your learning and knowledge-building. An unplanned effort to learn will lead to mental chaos. There is a time to learn, and you should plan how to learn. Browsing the Internet for topics of interest, participating in online workshops, completing courses, and reading selective manuals or books are ways to move forward in your learning journey.

- Books are a great source of learning and knowledge. They are not only your best friend, but they will open your mind to different knowledge domains.

- Finally, the better organized you are, the more you will learn. A good plan will help you to learn and gather information and knowledge without stress or anxiety.

Chapter 6

What Matters More Than Tools and Techniques

There are several consultants who collapse under work pressure. I personally have had numerous problems during my own consulting career. These problems are usually first with your team members, or team leader, or with someone on the client side. I have also seen similar problems faced by highly skilled consultants. Some of them could not complete their assignment, or they got replaced, or they had a very difficult time seeking cooperation from their client. Mind you, all these consultants have high technical skills and mastery over many tools, with more than 20 years of experience in the business.

So, why do they get into trouble? Arrogance is one of the main reasons why consultants get into trouble with clients. Humility, on the other hand, has just the opposite effect and helps consultants to build lasting long-term relationships. It is so simple, but why can't such intelligent people understand this? There are many reasons, but I believe it is mostly due to frustrations regarding some personal issues that they have harboured in their mind for long, or perhaps they were raised to be pompous and cannot correct themselves.

I will try to distil a few things that will help you meander through the complex consulting environment with relative ease and not get into trouble with your colleagues, team leaders, or anyone from the client's side.

Ability to Observe

Your ability to consciously observe everything going on around you is crucial. This ability will help you sense the mood and cope with the environment. There can be two scenarios, one where everyone agrees and shares information smoothly, and the other where you feel that people are uncomfortable in the collaboration, there's some sort of threat or racial tensions, or they are refraining from sharing information and data.

So, what do you need to observe to become more independent?

- When you are on the field, touring factories and production units or agricultural efforts and animal farms, you need to observe several things. For example, you must observe the size of the enterprise, how people are organized to produce, who controls the resources, what the work environment is like, the type of leadership, and what people say.
- In meetings, you must observe the seating arrangement. Who is chairing the meeting, who is present at the meeting, and the issues and agendas? During the meeting, observing the body language of the participants will give you important

information about the subtle responses of the participants on the issues discussed. This observation will help you to follow up on issues with different stakeholders in one-on-one meetings. Remember, almost 30% of the responses to issues in a meeting are non-verbal.

Know When to Keep Your Mouth Shut!

The ability to observe and give your input in a meeting or illustrate a point which will lead to an effective decision is a great skill. However, it is equally important to know when to keep quiet or withhold your views even if at that time you might think they are legitimate and important. It needs a lot of patience and discipline to be able to keep your mouth shut and not say things that are inappropriate in a discussion.

Your ability to pitch your views in a timely manner is something you will need to be conscious of and develop over time to have the highest impact. This ability is developed consciously and purposively through practice. I was once in North India at a huge trade fair held biannually. There, I attended several small group meetings. I came across an important delegate who attended all the meetings I had attended. I noticed that this gentleman would ask a question, and then, before the other participants could respond, he would state the answer. He did this so artfully that he was a master of making a point in a meeting. So, you must develop your own way to pitch your point in a meeting, so that it is considered useful and relevant by the other participants. Never speak to score points over the other participants. People are aware of such behaviour and the other members will not be happy about it.

How Much Information is Necessary to Share with Your Clients and Colleagues

A consultant works with many colleagues with different expertise and in various assignments, especially in consulting companies. In some cases, they work only on one assignment at a time. You will have a lot of information to share with different clients and colleagues. Is it important to share everything you know about a situation with your colleagues and clients? Should you vomit out everything you have learned from a situation or should you share information on a 'need-to-know' basis? Well, this is a matter of choice and balance.

There is always the case of information overload. Under highly stressful situations in a consulting environment where several things are happening simultaneously and you are competing with time to deliver and create outputs, you need to consider a more thoughtful and planned sharing of information. It should be well distilled and have enough clarity, such that when shared with colleagues, it will be easily comprehended and useful.

Ability to Ask a Good Question and the Right One

Questioning is more a science than an art! I know many of you may disagree. In consulting, whether a question is posed to the entire team or to a particular individual in the client organization is of high value, because if it is posed properly, the follow-up or leading questions will end up providing a wealth of information crucial for a successful assignment.

So, questioning in consultancy is a planned activity. You could plan your questioning in the following way. You can also personalize it.

- First, prepare mentally and then note down the different themes you plan to cover in your meeting, or interview.
- Second, sort out how much time you plan to invest in each issue, depending on the total duration of the introduction (this should exclude the time taken to exchange niceties).
- Third, under each theme/topic, list the type of questions you are going to ask. By type, I mean 'yes' or 'no' questions, the 'how,' 'why' and 'when' questions.

The timing of the question is also crucial. When should you ask the question during a discussion is a deciding factor as to whether you will get the right response. If your timing is wrong, then a lot of chaos can happen. Test this theory out by asking a question at the wrong time, and you will see what happens. Sometimes, it will annoy the other members in the meeting room who might consider you disruptive and your boss might think you need to change 'the software in your head!'

There was one team leader of mine, who was half Punjabi and half Chinese and a Malaysian citizen, who once told me after a meeting that I should change the software in my head. I then reflected and a few days later, I asked him why he had said that. He told me that I had asked relevant questions but had pitched them at the wrong time; I did that around four times during the entire meeting. When you pitch a question, especially an open-ended one, you need to be careful; this is where your ability to observe the meeting comes in handy.

You can miss out on a lot if you ask the wrong question, the wrong type of question, or if the timing of the question is wrong. Never ask a leading question at the beginning of your interview. A general, open-ended question is always appreciated, and people are comfortable answering it. Don't ask questions in a manner (speed and tone) which might appear to be like a court cross-examination of a witness, rather than a normal conversation seeking clarification and wanting new information.

Remember, questioning is always tagged by the respondent based on the tone of your voice, the way you spell out each word, your facial expression, hand gesticulation and your overall body language. Being mindful in meetings and interviews cannot be emphasized enough for consultants to be successful in their work.

Your Values will be Tested and Transacted

In the consulting business, your value is tested and exchanged among clients and the firm or organization you work with. Calvart Markham in his book, *The Art of Consultancy*, proposes the idea that an exchange of value takes place between the consultant, the consulting firm and the client. He proposes the following transactions in the exchange of value take place:

- *The individual consultant* transacts pay, development of consulting skills, technical competence, and sectoral experience with the consulting firm. With the client, the transaction is based on sectoral experience, expertise, and network.
- *The client,* on the other hand, transacts with the consulting firm capability problem orientation, and technology transfer. While with the individual consultant, it boils down to specialist knowledge, experience, and know-how.
- *The consulting firm* transacts free income, corporate expertise and credibility, and product development opportunities. The individual consultant transacts revenue, knowledge and business development.

Networking

Research has shown that it takes around seven seconds before a person develops a first impression when you meet someone for the first time. So, it's important to know how first impressions are actually formed. This usually happens during networking sessions held formally or informally.

This is an era where you will probably not be in the same job, or in the same position all your life and hence it is important to build relationships with people on the go to navigate your career path. This is where networking plays an important part in your professional life.

Building your knowledge tree involves expanding your knowledge and looking for new information. For this to happen, you need to know people. People are precious to any professional. They become your friends, your colleagues and your clients in the future. During networking, you must seek to build bridges and connect with like-minded people who can provide you with opportunities to learn through their association, have the potential to join you in a future mission, provide relevant information for a job, or even recommend a book or report.

This is an era of self-employment, and the world needs more freelance consultants than ever before for various kinds of industries in the private and public sectors. Is networking a waste of time? Well, the answer is NO! It is important to understand the nuances of networking. It is not about meeting people in a networking event and exchanging business cards; it is an effort to develop enduring relationships.

Dana Robinson, founding Partner of TechLaw, runs a course on LinkedIn called *The Ultimate Guide to Professional Networking.* She mentions during the training that you don't need a country club membership to network, or even attend events where you hand out and receive business cards. The training emphasizes that 'real networking is building relationships that will serve you for a lifetime. According to him, the old-school networking has changed over the last two decades.

Creating networks for life involves building productive relationships for life. Dana Robinson writes that networks are built with 'Tribes.' These are people having the same interests and doing similar things, and they are not found in obvious networking events, but on the sidelines of such events as near trade show events rather than at the event itself. Also in the training programmes, she introduces the concept of online 'clan,' forming families and superfamilies. She talks about these concepts under 'Elements of Organic Network Framework.'

Some of the other takeaways from this training are the following:

- Build relationships through empathy, and approach people the way you would like to be approached.
- Always give importance to the other person; listen carefully to what they say with keen interest and remember their names.
- Always follow the appropriate manners and do not ask personal questions.

- You need to write back to those you feel are part of your tribe within 24 to 48 hours of meeting them at any networking event.
- Remember that these people that you form a lifelong relationship with are 'awesome' and they should not be considered as your potential clients.
- Join online networking groups in your industry such as the Exporters Association, consulting networks, Network BNI, Vestege, EI, etc.

As a freelance consultant, you will have to constantly find work. Networks that you have developed will help you find work. Word of mouth from your colleagues and their recommendations will help you get work depending on your performance while you worked with them and the relationships that you have maintained with them over the years.

Therefore, remember to work well wholeheartedly, supporting your colleagues in consulting missions, because they will never forget how you behaved with them when you worked with them as a team. Since they will be your potential referees, always keep in touch with them, send them season's greetings, New Year's greetings, birthday wishes etc. These colleagues will be more important in helping you get jobs than people you meet during networking events.

Contractors and employers are the next lot of people that will offer you work. Public sector companies that hire your service will come back to you for more work if you have performed well in their previous assignments and have lived up to their expectations.

Scavenging for work requires a tremendous effort that many consultants must put in to acquire an assignment with contracting companies. This entails sending your CVs to many companies, browsing job websites, Dev Net, Donor websites and similar places. Also, apply via LinkedIn ads. From my experience, if you are a consultant from the South, your chances of landing an assignment will not be as good when compared to your peers from the North, partly because most donor funding and contracting companies are from the North, and they trust that consultants from their region are more likely to deliver results. They like to give work to citizens of countries that have provided resources to these organizations through shares.

Copycat Prowling

Copycats are all over the place in the consulting business, both in the private and public sectors. Never share an idea with anyone in private. You will suddenly see this colleague blurting the same idea out in a meeting or including it in his/her report. It is better to hold on to your ideas and spell them out in a meeting in front of your colleagues and clients so that the ideas are recorded to be yours, and later you can also mention the same in your report.

There will be many people who will attempt to pick your brains for ideas. Be aware of them and stay at arm's length from them. These are desperate people who have weak mental capabilities to think and have all along made their way by stealing the ideas of others. They will drain you. In our business, all intellectual property and copyrights that are often written about are a farce and they are often violated with impunity by these very constituents who are the proponents of such rights.

Disillusionment

You are likely to be disillusioned in this profession at some point in your career. The slow pace at which things happen around you, the difficulty in acquiring data and information, your uncooperative colleagues, racism, and an abusive and moody team leader or colleague, are challenges that can make you feel disillusioned.

I remember one mission I had worked on in Papua, New Guinea, where we were working with a group from a multilateral bank. Here, we had a team member from Australia who refused to speak with an Indian consultant just because he was not white and Anglo-Saxon. They completely ignored the Asian consultant throughout the mission. You will come across such situations but don't be disillusioned.

I had a bad experience myself and I was totally disillusioned; that day I told my wife that I would resign from my profession immediately. This was in December 2011. A new country manager was going to take charge of the office in India. I was working in a cabin that was dank and dusty and I couldn't bear the smell every morning when I came in to work. So, every day I would burn an incense stick. The cabin had glass doors through which I saw my Italian country manager walk straight into my cabin and introduce me to the new English country manager. At this first introduction, he asked me, "Are your very religious?" I was absolutely stunned. "Why do you ask?" I retorted. He had asked because of the incense stick burning next to my desk. He never believed that I was not religious until I left the organization to become a freelance consultant. Later, in the years to come, one of his colleagues who I had worked with, informed him that I was a great whisky drinker, and I gave a fuck about religion and race; he changed his mind about me.

So be careful how you judge people so that you are neither guilty nor disillusioned. Don't be disillusioned when people judge you or are racist without hardly knowing you. Take it in your stride as there are mean and good people on our planet. You need to be with the good guys. Theoretically, race and religion have no place in our profession, but unfortunately, the reality is quite different. You need to compose your mind and spirit to fight this with tact, knowledge, diplomacy and skill so that you are above them. If you don't, the toxic environment created by toxic people and bullies will burn you down and you will be damaged and sick forever.

Don't be Replaced by Artificial Intelligence

This might sound a bit crazy, but there is every possibility in the future that you might be replaced by AI. Experts believe that soon, with a new era of specialization where you need to make a living as an expert, there will be several jobs taken over by AI. We have seen what AI can do in so many fields including core areas of programming languages and in architecture, which is one of the most creative sciences. The following are AI tools that are used for automation today: Scikit Learn, TensorFlow, PyTorch, CNTK, Caffe, Apache MXnet, Keras, OpenNN, AutoML, and H20. You should check them out on the net.

Therefore, there is every reason to first build expertise as a consultant which will be difficult to replace with AI or have a broad knowledge and skill base such that it is almost impossible for AI to replace. Experts are of the opinion that the narrower your knowledge and skill set, the more likely that it will be replaced by AI, and you will lose your job.

Mindbench.com in his blog written in 2022 titled *How will the AI revolution affect management consulting?* he says, "As AI continues to be implemented within the industry, it's going to disrupt some of the patterns we've become accustomed to. For many, this means you'll have to shift the goalposts and alter the ways in which you bring value to clients."

It concludes that many companies are creating a hybrid work environment to work in conjunction with AI. They are planning to use AI to train employees. Consulting companies that have high knowledge regarding the capabilities of AI are trying to develop consultants with 'sharpened human qualities' such as critical thinking and emotional intelligence, to build competitive advantage for the future.

A global survey on AI conducted by McKinsey titled *The State of AI in 2022 – and a Half Decade in Review,* found the expansion of AI technology, wherein organizations using AI have plateaued between 50 to 60% over the past years. The five-year review shows that AI adoption has more than doubled, with 20% of respondents in 2017 having adopted AI in at least one business area. In 2022, the figure stood at 50%, peaking at 58% in 2019.

The survey also found that among the AI capabilities, the most commonly used by companies are natural language text understanding, robotic process automation and computer vision.

In addition, the survey found that AI was used for functional activities, where AI capabilities are used for service operations followed by product and/or service development, marketing and sales, and risk. The survey also found an increase in the investment in AI. Around 40% of the respondents reported more than 5% of their digital budget on AI and 63% of respondents reported that in the next three years from the date the survey was undertaken, they expect their companies to invest more in AI.

It is time for freelance consultants to start investing in training to learn AI technology. Recently, I came across an Indian Institute of Technology graduate who had published his training course for anyone interested in learning Chat GPT and AI technology, as he believes that AI will be the next generation of IT skills that one will have to learn to survive in the job market and solve the client's problems.

Experts believe that AI will replace most of the research-oriented activities in management consulting. Consulting companies are using AI in various ways. For example, Deloitte is using AI to automate processes to mimic human decision-making, interactions and judgements to drive results at different levels of business.

In the consulting industry, AI will take over work mainly related to quantitative research initially. For example, it will take over survey data collection, data cleaning and analysis.

However, it is highly unlikely that AI will be able to replace freelance consultants, because they provide highly specialized services through specialized skill sets, using their experience, intuitions and creativity, especially in the field of design, creative art in interior design, well-being and insights that allow the client to make optimal decisions. Furthermore, clients prefer to work with freelancers who can provide personal attention and build productive relationships and rapport.

Around 20% of freelancers think that AI will replace them. One survey shows a positive trend where 55% of the respondents believe that AI will not be able to replace freelancers. AI has high potential in the freelance industry to support data analysis, project management and communication. Repetitive tasks can be undertaken by AI which will reduce time and provide beneficial insights. Instead of replacing human freelancing, it will support freelance consultants in accomplishing certain tasks and hence AI is unlikely to replace human freelance consultants.

The blog titled *Freelancing in the Cultural and Creative Industries*, mentions that freelancers make up 33% of the CCI workforce, and 70% of the workforce in the Performing Arts industry are self-employed freelancers. The value of the CCI is USD 2.25 billion. In Europe, the CCI represents a market value of 253 billion euros, which is 1.7% of the European GDP. In 2019, freelancers, creative businesses, organizations, and creators generated a turnover of 643 billion euros which was equal to 4.4% of the European economy that year. Therefore, the creative industry is safe from the infiltration of AI and the erosion of jobs for creative freelancers.

According to another very interesting blog by Talent Desk titled *Why AI Can't Replace Freelancers and Take Over Jobs* dated March 21, 2023, AI cannot replace freelancers in the creative industry for the following reasons:

- There is a high probability of duplication of content as there are millions of people requesting AI to provide the same content and there is the risk of duplication.
- The AI information may not be timely and relevant. For example, the GTP data is only up to date till 2021. Hence, if the information is not updated, you will get old content from AI bots.
- AI lacks originality. It cannot come up with original thinking and will produce results based on what is analyzed and fed into the system. It uses algorithms and processes the data, leading to an intelligent combination of information to come up with some content, as if working like a human brain. Originality and original thinking are missing!
- AI lacks experience, although it has a vast amount of knowledge. Unlike human beings, they have a limited capacity to learn from successes and failures, but I reckon they will be able to do that in the future. Regardless, I don't see how they will be able to replace the experience gathered by a freelance consultant.

I am optimistic that the freelancing industry will gain from the development of AI and learn to work with AI to solve the complex problems of clients. In the creative industry such as architecture, fine arts, and interior décor, freelance consultants can work together with AI to come up with solutions that will provide greater satisfaction to clients.

Make Your Presence Felt

In every assignment, you must be able to make your presence felt, not through arrogant behaviour and showing off your knowledge, but by being supportive and generous with information, listening, and helping whenever you can. Furthermore, small gestures also matter, such as getting a glass of water for your colleague when you are dining together, sharing meals with your work colleagues, and providing and sharing useful insights of the day over coffee, lunch or dinner.

You must make your presence felt with the client by communicating effectively with them regarding the work in progress and deliverables completed through high-quality presentations. Look for opportunities during your assignments to train, coach and mentor members of the client side with your advanced expertise.

Your Success Framework

Success in any field needs effort that is carefully planned, thought out and executed. Aside from effort and hard work, it is based on a success recipe, which is either developed by a coach or mentor or by yourself. Hence, your success in a consulting assignment needs a framework just like consulting problems need a framework for resolution. I have mentioned the 4 S Method and the three major paths to solving problems in the previous sections. For a consulting assignment to be successful you need a framework. I propose the following framework:

Fitness is the **core of this framework**. You need to be physically and mentally fit, be able to communicate effectively and build relationships, analyze data and information and deliver timely outputs and deliverables. I remember working with a UN Country Director in Indonesia; I learned numerous things from him. He was a fit ex-rugby player and a great swimmer. He told me once how important it was for us to keep fit when we hit the road. Especially when on the road, away from home, it is extremely important to keep fit physically and mentally by exercising – hitting the gym, taking a long walk, running or swimming. This advice stuck with me and from then on, I tried to keep fit while on a mission, sometimes just doing free hand exercises in my hotel room. I exercise regularly when I am at home, working or not working.

If you are not fit, you will probably be less alert, lack confidence and the ability to communicate effectively to build productive relationships, collect and analyze data and information and provide a coherent argument, addressing critical issues and providing flawless recommendations.

Communication and building relationships are **the left base of the success framework pyramid.** To be able to communicate effectively with colleagues, team members and clients, and to build lasting relationships, especially with clients and the contracting team, is the major foundation for success in a consulting assignment.

Data and information analysis are the right base of the pyramid, and the next foundation for success at the bottom of the success pyramid. It requires energy and determination to be able to collect the necessary data and relevant information to analyze. You need to choose the correct analytical methods that will provide the information and recommendations that are critical and relevant to the objective functions of the assignment. The way you set the hypothesis or identify the issue for issue-driven analysis or design thinking analysis, will all matter as regards the success of your assignment or mission.

Timely outputs and deliverables – Almost all clients need timely mission or assignment outputs and deliverables. If you are consulting for the UN or the EU, you will be given a fixed amount of time to come up with the deliverables. You will have to furnish a work plan to the Team Leader or if you are leading you will have to prepare your own work plan integrated with the work plan of your respective team members. **Timely submission of deliverables in the form of assignment reports and work completion reports and study reports is at the top of the assignment success pyramid.**

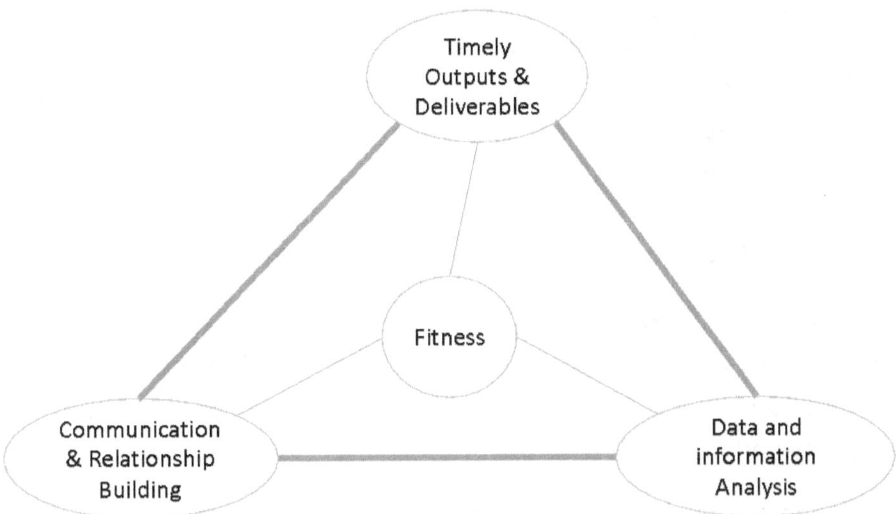

Brand Building and Marketing

Most consultants that I have met work independently, never really making a conscious effort to market their firm or their work. Their profile exists only on LinkedIn. In recent years, I have seen consultants using Instagram to post some of their ongoing work such as field visits and visits to the factory. The trend has been set by the younger generation of consultants to market their work on social media.

Investing in marketing was not considered important because it involves a lot of work, especially in the private and public sectors. The consultants from the north were mostly from the donor countries and hence it was easy to get work, while those from the south, because of their networking ability and good relations with their colleagues from the north, got work from them.

These days, there is still work in the private sector, and you could get work through word of mouth. It is however becoming increasingly difficult, depending on which country you are based in. For example, I have an American friend who is married to an Indian and he was in India for a while. He was able to get training consulting and strategy consulting work in small and medium-scale industries very easily through recommendations and word of mouth. He had to move to Brazil due to some personal problems in India, and although his quality of life was better in Sao Paulo, it was difficult for him to get work as a freelance consultant. Just a few days ago, he informed me that he is going to move to Saudi Arabia with his family as the prospects of getting a job in consulting firms there were much better.

You must use social media to market and showcase your work. In addition, focus on building your personal brand by perhaps publishing and posting blogs on your area of expertise on LinkedIn, Facebook or Twitter. The other way and perhaps the best way to do it is to publish a book.

Create something during a consulting assignment to ensure the clients and the contracting company will remember you. For example, write a programme to analyze a set of data, or train clients in a specific software that will add value to their work process. In the field of infrastructure, designing a good road, bridge and other infrastructure will always contribute to your brand building. There are high-flying experts such as the man who designed the Burj Khalifa in Dubai; he built his brand through his work. I am sure that if there is another tall building that is going to be built anywhere in the world, he will be a much sought-after expert.

I worked for a private sector enterprise and a popular brand selling plant nutrients. The company was conducting 60% of its business on credit and 40% was cash-based. I designed a small computer program in Excel to track the outstanding credit, collection duration, delinquency rates and recovery rates for a specific area office. The entire company came to know my work. People appreciate and remember when you create something useful, especially if they are your clients.

As a freelancer, you must build your personal brand. It is vital that you do! If you have talent, you must show your talent and work. One book that influenced me to write this book was Show *Your Work! 10 Ways to Share Your Creativity and Get Discovered* by Austin Kleon. Towards the end of the book Austin writes, "Go online and post what you are working on right now with the tag # Show Your Work." He is indeed passionate about the importance of showcasing your work. In the book, he offers an alternative method for those who don't like the idea of self-promotion.

He in fact lays out a process of brand building, where he recommends writing daily and sending out a dispatch every day. He goes on to underscore the importance of a domain name where he suggests that when buying a domain name, if your name is common, or you don't like your name, come up with a pseudonym or alias and register. He says that you should not think of your website as a 'self-promotion machine' but as a 'self-invention machine.'

I suggest that for the purpose of brand building, a freelancer needs to do the following:

Build a website – Build a website with reviews of your work, samples of your work, photographs, professional conferences and meetings that you have attended for people to essentially view your work. You must pick the right platform, use WordPress, Swarespace or Wix. Use a proper CMS – which will give you independence, keep the costs low and allow you to work with speed. Choose any one of the following: Word Press, Drupal, and Joomla, as the first 10 million top websites use these Content Management Systems. Chose a domain name and select your host and web hosting company. I suggest that you get help from IT experts who have installed several websites.

Use social media – To stand out as a freelancer, you must use social media to your advantage. You can showcase your knowledge and skills, and samples of your work visually by posting blogs with still photographs, or even videos of your work. If you are working in sales and marketing or in the creative industry, then opening an Instagram account to market your products and your designs, etc. is imperative.

Personal logo for your business card and website – As a freelancer, it is important to have a personal logo, which should be used on your website and business card.

Planning -You Plan, and God Laughs

"If your plan doesn't work change the plan, do not change the goal."

– Anonymous

Normally, religious people believe that your life's plan is designed by God Almighty. I am a great believer in this, and surely your life is steered in various directions by God Almighty. Here, I want to focus on the daily planning of your work and activities. Simultaneously, you should prepare annual plans and set personal and professional milestones.

For example, you could set the following milestones: I will lose 5 kgs by March; I will complete the assignment for X Donor by May; I will go on a vacation in August to the Maldives with my girlfriend; I will get married in December before Christmas. Personal and professional plans go hand in hand. This is life and you must have a plan for everything you do. This will reduce stress and contribute to your well-being.

To plan your activities, you need to know what you want to achieve during the day. It is useful to put it down on paper so that you can visually see what you want to achieve and whether it is possible to achieve it during the day. The first thing to remember is that whatever you want to achieve for that day, even if you wish to work for twelve hours, it should be realistic.

Once you have identified your activities, you must allocate time to start and finish the activities. You must take the help of your colleagues if you need to find out what must be completed and submitted for that day to the client or team leader. All this might seem like common sense, but I can assure you that this method is not commonly used by everyone. Planning your day as a consultant is the key to your success in accomplishing your daily goals.

Once you have allocated the time slots to complete your work you could follow the *Pomodoro Technique of time management* for work. This technique was developed by an entrepreneur named Francesco Cirello in 1980. As a university student, he used a tomato-shaped kitchen timer to schedule his studies. He tried several time intervals and found that he could optimally stay focused for around 25 minutes and then he needed a break of three to five minutes before he resumed work.

He proposed the following steps:

- Identify a task or tasks that you need to complete.
- Set a timer for 25 minutes.
- Work on a task with no distractions.
- When the alarm sounds, take a 5-minute break.
- Repeat the process three more times.
- Take a longer, 30-minute break, and start again.

Now that you know how to plan your day, you also need to plan your week and year. In consulting, weekly planning can be done based on how you schedule your work with the client. However, the yearly planning is difficult as the 12 months planning horizon could be busted with unforeseen events in today's fast-paced world. I would stick to a weekly plan prepared based on a discussion with the client, agreeing on a timetable for the deliverables.

You need to bear in mind that daily plans are useful, but these are more easily achieved if you have built some good habits pertaining to managing time. Planning may sometimes fail, but you will always win with good work habits and time management. So, you need to review your good habits regularly, and you must make it a habit to plan your day and make it a habit to follow a time management technique.

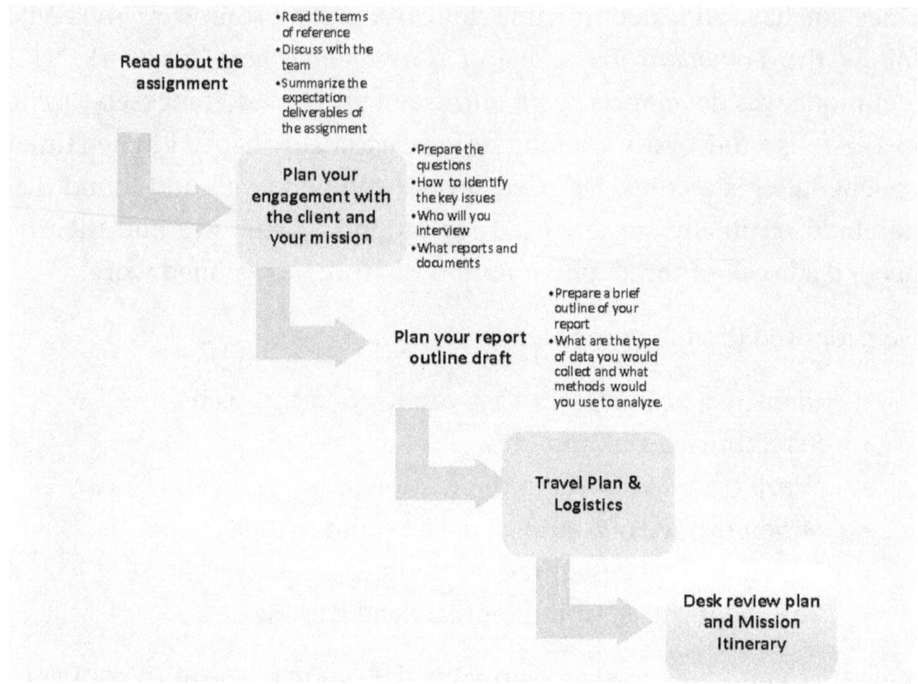

Working in a Team

"Treat others as you would like to be treated."

– Anonymous

What are teams in consulting? Well, like all teams, a consulting team is formed based on the nature of the assignment. There is a team leader and a set of consultants. This team is temporary; like a project management team, it is dismantled or adjourned after the completion of the assignment. You might be in a situation where you might need to work in two or more teams during a certain period, or during the whole year. If this is the case, then your challenges will be greater, as you must cope with different team dynamics.

I need to remind you here that each team is not the same and each team goes through the processes of forming, storming, norming, performing and eventually ending the team. Depending on what stage the team is at, it will have its own dynamics.

When the team is formed, the team members meet and come together and introduce themselves. In the nineties, the teams physically met, but nowadays, it is common to form the team virtually.

The next stage is storming, where team members try to know one another and struggle to work together, finding the experience difficult.

Then you have the norming stage where the members get to know one another better and set working rules and are more functional as a team.

The next is the performing stage where the team achieves results, delivers outputs and is a high-performing team.

You must learn to be a good team member. The following are a few key tips to navigating the team environment in consulting, especially when you are working in a multicultural and multigenerational team:

- Remember the names of your team members and pronounce them correctly. Cross-check with team members if you are unsure of the right pronunciation. Most people don't like their names being mispronounced. When I started work, I was terrible at pronouncing names correctly, but I worked hard to ensure that I got their names right!
- Respect your team members by understanding cultural nuances and differences. You should however not compromise on your own culture to assimilate with another culture. Do not disrespect other cultures, like for example, their choice of food, drinks or the way they eat. Although there is a common denominator of

decency, there is a subtle difference that needs to be taken note of and respected.

- Listen to what team members have to say carefully without interruption.
- Support team members with information, documents, slide decks and reports.
- Try to have meals together or coffee.
- Be open-minded about the ideas of others; be assertive but do not quarrel.
- Attend all team meetings and be flexible.
- Support team members with their work so that team outputs are not delayed, and you have timely deliverables.

Self-auditing your experience in the team is a good habit once the mission is over. You should note what you did best as a team member and what more you could have done. What worked in the team and what didn't? This structured reflection will help you to pick up best practices and lessons, which you will be able to use in your next assignment and improve your performance and contribute to the performance of the next team you will be working with.

Values are Tested

Individual values are important in the consulting practice or profession. As a freelance consultant, your values will be tested while you are on an assignment throughout the mission/assignment. They will be tested by your team members and by the client.

Identify your values. If you are unsure, think about what values you hold that will help you to work professionally as a freelance consultant. Write down these values you hold close to your heart and make sure your decisions are based on or guided by these values. Value-led behaviour is authentic, and you will be respected by your clients and colleagues

Walk the talk to demonstrate that you have the grit and strong values that drive you to do what you do and say what you say.

Summary

- Freelance consulting needs more than just technical skills to be successful; you much know how to handle an assignment and perform effectively.
- Having the ability to observe the visual landscape such as seating arrangements in a meeting, interactions between colleagues and clients and their body language, is indeed very important.
- You must learn how to pitch, and when to keep your mouth shut. It is a unique tactic you will have to develop with practice. You will be more effective as a consultant and gain the respect of your clients.
- You must learn judiciousness in providing information to clients and colleagues – sometimes following the 'need-to-know' basis is good and sometimes it's not. The information, when provided, must be specific, credible and useful.
- Learn the art of questioning. You must practice the art of asking the right question at the right time.
- Networking is essential for a freelance consultant. Your efforts to network should be aimed at building a long-lasting relationship; it is not about developing your client base, or just introducing yourself with your business card. You will find people from your sector and those with similar interests on the sidelines of networking events. Look for them!
- In this profession, you must share your original thoughts and ideas in official settings where your ideas are recorded. There are many people who will take your idea and call it their own. Remember, everyone wants to prove their worth in a competitive environment such as consulting.
- You are likely to be disillusioned in this profession often or sometimes. You must stick to your values and find out the root cause of the challenges you face and reflect on the situation objectively. This will help you to remain calm and confident.

- Choose your field of expertise such that your knowledge and skills cannot be replaced by AI. Experts claim that if your skill base is very narrow, for example, writing computer programs, then it is likely to be replaced by AI. Developing a broad-based skill set is very useful. Soon, technical experts as consultants will have to work interactively with AI to deliver results for your clients. This is already happening in the field of architecture and medical science.

- I have shared a Success Framework for you to use. You can also develop a framework of your own to be effective and successful in your consulting assignments.

- Most freelance consultants that I have met don't really market their firms or work. They usually get work through word of mouth. They are usually referred by colleagues (in most cases), donors, contractors, or a government ministry. They are sometimes scouted by HR firms. It is important to market a bit of your work using social media. Public memory is short-lived! However, someone in the industry or sector will remember you.

- You need to cultivate the habit of daily planning. This habit will be useful during your assignments. You could have annual plans with specific personal and professional milestones to achieve. Planning your assignment is crucial for effective and efficient consulting and for the successful completion of an assignment.

- Teams are an indispensable part of any consulting assignment – you will hardly get to work alone. You are either working with a team formed by the contractor, or your firm or you are working with a client's team. Your ability to work with team members, both multicultural and multigenerational, is vital to your success as a consultant.

Chapter 7

Look After Yourself

"Eat well, read books, study yourself, expand your mind, do better and get better. Last but not least, remember you are your greatest investment."

– Warren Buffet

Have you met a burnt-out person? Do you know how a burnt-out person behaves? Do you know anyone who is burnt out? A burnt-out person is one who is nervous, often sick with either blood pressure or diabetes at an early stage in his or her life, depressed and lacking in energy and enthusiasm to work. It is sad to see and meet people suffering from burnout due to organizational and work pressure.

Work burnout happens because of two factors: The first is internal and the other is external. The internal factor is generally when a person does not look after himself or herself. The external factor could be a toxic work environment, a bullying boss, and racist colleagues. As a freelance consultant, you can easily get burnt out and become permanently sick. It can happen to anyone, trust me. Here, I want to give you some tips that will make you physically and mentally strong and burn-proof!!

If you love yourself, you will look after yourself. Nothing is more important than your life and your health. Not even your girlfriend, wife, kids, your boss, and job. Let me give you the following tips to improve your effectiveness as a consultant and simultaneously improve your well-being:

Get Yourself Organized

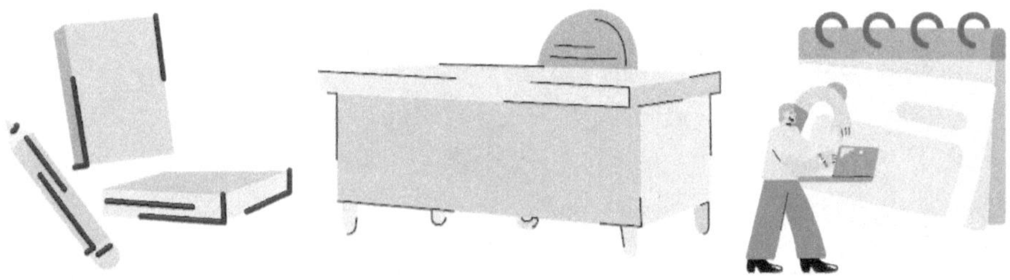

Being organized is the first step towards effectiveness and stress reduction. You must organize your entire life in general. First, focus on your health. Have an annual health check, take your medication and dietary advice seriously and follow everything systematically. Incorporate meditation and exercise in your life and pursue your hobbies. Subsequently, you need to organize your house, wardrobe, kitchen, and workspace. In other words, declutter your house and remove all forms of clutter.

Organizing your work means that you have a good library, a good filing system, and a good computer filing system. You should have enough light to work in your office, and heating and cooling systems. You need to buy an ergonomic chair, a proper working desk with table lamps, a laptop stand, external keyboards, a desktop computer, a good camera, a high-quality blog microphone and headsets to conduct online video chats. You need to have ample colour pens, post-it paper, notepads, document markers and other necessary stationary. You should buy a good journal, preferably a bullet journal, and a good physical calendar in sync with the Google or Outlook calendar that you have already installed on your computer. Being organized is very important for high effectiveness!

Manage Your Energy and Your Time

You need to manage your energy very well. Carving out time for rest in your schedule to go out for a walk or to a coffee shop to pick up a drink, is essential. Make sure you take time to drink fresh water while you work at frequent intervals and during long meetings. This will keep you hydrated and help you to be alert and awake. Of course, if you have an opportunity to have an 11:00 a.m. snack or a 3:00 p.m. snack, have it, especially a bowl of fresh salad with fresh juice or coffee.

It is equally good to take a short nap or meditate to manage your energy, which is essential when you are working under high pressure and in a demanding assignment.

All freelance consultants need to read this book by Jim Loehr and Toney Schwartz titled *The Power of Full Engagement – Managing Energy, Not Time, Is the Key to High Performance and Personal Renewal*. They conclude that energy is the most important 'currency' for high performance, and one must be physically and emotionally energized, mentally focused and spiritually aligned. They concluded the following:

The capacity to perform is based on *"one's ability to expand and recovery energy."*

"Every thought, feeling and action has an energy consequence."

"Energy is the most important individual and organizational resource." (Page:197)

This is so profound. Several gadgets and schedulers are available to manage time, but we have ignored the whole idea of managing energy. The energy they are referring to is both your physical and mental energy. In my view, both these energies are linked to one another. There is a limit to your will to work if your physical energy is depleted. You may be fit as a fiddle, but you may not be able to perform optimally if your emotional or mental energy is low – it will affect your concentration and your communication. Remember, freelancing is a very high-paced activity. Most often, you are paid for your time, and you must work at a ferocious speed to meet set deadlines. I have never met a client that is not demanding.

Reduce Stress

By focusing on matching your time with your good habits, it reduces your time spent on bad habits such as surfing the net or checking your phone often. To reduce stress, you must know what needs to be avoided more than what needs to be done. This will help you understand your productivity threshold.

Reduce your stress by taking a walk, taking short breaks during work, having a chat with your colleague during lunch, going for a run after work, hitting the gym, doing yoga, or going to the cinema and enjoying a bag of popcorn! Find a way to reduce stress. According to Jim Loehr and Toney Schwartz, "We are oscillatory beings in an oscillatory universe. Rhythmicity is our inheritance." This statement is profound. According to them, oscillation happens at the basic level of our being, so we need to understand that a healthy pattern of activity and rest increases our capacity to engage fully, have maximum performance and remain healthy.

How to Stick to the To-Do List

This is a bit difficult to do. I would rather you take up bullet journaling. This will make your life more organized, and you will be able to manage both your time and energy as proposed by the founder of the Bullet Journal method, Ryder Carroll. The author promises that "The Bullet Journal method will help you accomplish more by working less." It will help you identify and focus on what is meaningful by stripping away what is meaningless.

Journaling for a consultant is a good habit as it helps you track your thoughts and actions and is a basis for regular reflection and review of your work and your day. The author shows that the whole process is about intentionality, which is a subset of productivity and mindfulness. He mentions that it will help to declutter your mind and objectively examine your thoughts from a distance.

A Bullet Journal is made with your hand and the content is handwritten. According to Ryder Carroll, writing helps us to think and feel at the same time. Hence, it comprises writing and reflecting. The journal can be organized to record task lists, and plans and take notes. So, you need a notebook and a pen and then you prepare the journal accordingly. Nowadays, you can buy readymade bullet journals on Amazon or Flipkart.

You can list tasks that are broken down into sub-tasks, allot space for tick-marking to indicate completion, migrate tasks to another day and schedule tasks.

The author provides a guide to creating the journal in the following way:

- Prepare an index page with the content and page numbers.
- A future log records future tasks that will be completed within a month.
- A monthly log comprises a list of tasks to be completed for the month with the corresponding timeline.
- A daily log is maintained to rapidly log your thoughts throughout the day.
- A rapid log captures your priorities and thoughts with symbols, events, notes, and tasks.

Together, they are called a collection, which is a modular building block used to store related content. Ryder Carroll recommends the monthly process of filtering out meaningless content from your notebook.

Taking smart notes is a skill and Sonke Ahrens in her book *How to Take Smart Notes* explains that experienced academic readers take notes by reading a text with questions in their minds. They question the content and see what is and is not mentioned in the text. The author mentions four underlying principles and explains these principles in great detail. Of these principles, two are applicable to freelance consultants:

a. *Writing is the only thing that matters* – Students of research demonstrate what they have learned and their ability to think critically and develop ideas.

b. *Simplicity is Paramount* – According to her, the simplicity of an idea makes it powerful. It is important that we take notes on ideas that occur as we engage with clients. She says that if we write fleeting notes which are only reminders of information in any kind of way, it will land up in the trash. This is a good point to keep in mind in terms of the intentionality of writing notes during the assignment, which will usually be a part of your analytical report. Most things that freelance consultants note are rough, undistilled or uncleaned qualitative data. Normally, they fall under certain thematic areas. There are notes kept separately to be used later as they are considered of high value, and there will be temporary notes used during the project and subsequently archived in the project file.

You should make journaling a habit. You could write your journal at night before going to bed and review your plan and tasks for the day in the morning, taking rapid notes or doing rapid logging during the day. I highly recommend that you go through this book if you want to get a good grip on journaling. There are numerous YouTube videos but do not watch these videos before reading this book.

Avoid Worst Practices and Embrace Best Practices

In the consulting business, you will come across the phrase 'best practices' frequently in your reports and conversations. There is however very little mention of the worst practices. There are many consultants who use processes and methods which are old, or arduous and drain the energy of the team.

These are essentially the worst practices. You could brainstorm the worst practices if you have some experience in consulting. We often fail to identify worst practices which are omnipresent, and nobody talks about them. If you want to be a smart consultant, then avoid the worst practices; it is only when you do this can you embrace the best practices.

Bitch But Don't Ditch

"Gentle and forgiving thoughts crystalize into habits of gentleness, which solidify into protective and preservative circumstances."

– James Allen in As a Man Thinketh

Speaking ill about anyone is not a nice thing. However, in consulting, a bit of bitching about the client, team member, team leader or project manager, does go on. It is better to avoid such criticisms and instead have a one-on-one with the person concerned and clarify everything. Sometimes, bitching could involve small banter over a meal but don't ever ditch your team member or team leader in front of a client. Speak highly of your colleagues and the team leader in front of your client.

Ditching someone during an engagement or a mission means that you don't provide information to the person, don't share documents and data, exclude them in important emails, and worst still, ignore the person completely during a meeting. You can bitch a bit but don't ditch.

This reminds me of a very profound statement made by Marcus Aurelius in his book *Meditations*:

"Judge every word and deed which are according to nature to be fit for thee; and be not diverted by the blame which follows from any people nor by their word, but if a thing is good to be done or said, do not consider it unworthy of thee. For those persons have their peculiar leading principle and follow their peculiar movement; which things do not thou regard, but go straight on, following thy own nature and the common nature; and the way of both is one." (Page: 760)

Your ability to be able to critique the right way is a skill that needs practice. Always check your ability to identify your blind spots when it comes to receiving feedback and critiquing others.

First, the emotional response to the person is more important than the feedback itself and second, how does the person giving the feedback treat you? So, you need to be aware of these two triggers when receiving feedback from colleagues and team members. This means you should be more concerned about the relationship with the person than the feedback itself. In situations like this, our response is more on a personal level than the feedback.

The other aspect is that the feedback does not align with your identity, where you perhaps feel that it is an attack on your competence and integrity. In such a situation, you are likely to overreact and be on the defensive. A person with a growth mindset usually recognizes these triggers and they treat feedback as a coaching or mentoring session rather than an evaluation of your action and behaviour. A boss of mine, who was nasty overall, always spoke one truth: Receiving feedback is like receiving gold! You need to separate your emotions from the facts. If the person still has negative feedback it should be treated factually and action should be taken accordingly. The emotional component should be removed while acting on the feedback.

You need to understand the intent of the feedback to handle it better. You need to first understand what the intended evaluation, coaching and appreciation is. You need to listen to the body of the feedback, and while you are doing this, listen to your own emotions and ask for clarification. Then, try to explain the situation in your own language, diagnosing and describing it. Clarify everything and discuss who is going to do what and the follow-up action plan. Make sure the person understands how you are going to go about it. The other person, who could be your boss, team leader or colleague, will feel valued. They will then have a more positive impact on your life and your relationship with them will be strengthened.

Crack a Problem and Don't Hack

"Consider that men will do the same things nevertheless, even though thou shoulderst burst."

– Marcus Aurelius

When you are a consultant working in the public or private sector, you are essentially solving a problem for the government, or a private sector company. You cannot and are not expected to solve or crack the problem in a consulting assignment all by yourself on the first attempt. You will participate with a team of experts to crack the problem. You need to understand your role and examine facts, data and information that are relevant to solving a particular piece of the problem. Your action in this regard must be progressive and not regressive. You will need to be innovative, authentic and original.

However, many consultants have this tendency to retrofit solutions based on their past experiences with a similar problem; and this is a hack. Hacking a solution will not solve the problem, because even if the problem may appear to be similar, it is under a different context and circumstance.

Keep the Big Picture in Your Bag

Consulting is an intense activity. You need focus, concentration and energy to achieve results and make your client happy. In this endeavour, you are dealing with data, information and impressions, diving deep into an issue or problem and in this pursuit, you may lose sight of the big picture.

You will be able to develop the big picture when you understand the 'situation' and 'problem' or 'complication.' Thereafter, as you get into this deep exercise by framing the appropriate questions, you must keep going back to the big picture, or else you will meander away from the main issues and address issues that are not significant in solving the problem or the complication.

Good Health Recipe for a Consultant

A consultant needs to be in good health. Firstly, the job demands your energy and attention span. An unhealthy person will not have the energy to sustain the demands of various activities and will perhaps become sicker. It will certainly affect his/her health. There are many consultants who work very well, delivering the best possible results despite suffering from autoimmune diseases such as high blood pressure and diabetes. So, how do they manage their health so well?

It is because of the following reasons: They are highly knowledgeable and skilled in their field of expertise. They work out regularly, eat mindfully and get at least seven to eight hours of sleep. They invest in productive time with their family and have a few good friends they are in touch with. They have silent moments for reflection, usually have a mentor or they mentor others and are charitable. They read a lot and surf the net for new information to be on top of things in their field of expertise. They dress well and save money to be financially secure.

Workout – Exercising is one of the best ways to keep fit. If you combine this with meditation, the impact is even better. I remember my colleague telling one day while we were on a mission in Indonesia, "You need to hit the gym especially when you are on the road." I still remember his advice to this today. You could go for a walk for around 20 minutes to an hour, or go for a run for around 30 minutes to an hour. You can do free hand exercises in your hotel room or at the gym. You can do strength training in a gym with weights. All these activities in combination with intelligent healthy eating habits will keep you fit.

Eat mindfully – I have never come across a consultant who works in his own state or province. If he is working in his country, he is probably working in a different province where the food is completely different from what he is used to eating at home. Or else, he is overseas, in a country where the food is again completely different. Under these circumstances, it is important to eat in clean hotels and restaurants and avoid street foods as much as possible. Secondly, you should eat what suits your body.

Selecting the right food from the menu and eating mindfully are vital to keeping in good shape and health during a consulting assignment. Never try to please or impress your host, or your team members and eat something that you are not used to, or else you will be in big trouble! Just eat carefully and only those food items that suit your tummy. While you are travelling, it is better to avoid eating at roadside motels. Carry bananas with you. Bananas are a hygienic fruit and will keep you full and energized.

Sleep – There are many important things that happen when we sleep. The biological process entails the repair of body cells, the restoration of energy, and the release of hormones and proteins. The brain gets rid of toxic waste and stores new information. New nerve cells are formed which helps proper brain functioning. Sleep deprivation can ruin all this completely. You will notice that sleep-deprived people are incoherent, irritating and sluggish.

According to the Mayo Clinic, a normal adult needs seven or more hours of sleep each night. Those adults who sleep for five hours each night on a regular basis will be sleep deprived. Sleep deprivation causes bodily injury and could lead to heart disease, kidney disease, high blood pressure, diabetes, stroke, obesity and depression. While on a consulting assignment, you usually get less than seven hours of sleep due to the demand to perform and deliver within the scheduled time. If you plan your tasks properly you can schedule at least seven hours of sleep. When you are not working, you should make sure you get more than seven hours of sleep each night.

Family time, if you have one – The family is the centre of gravity for most married men and women and even those who are single. Family is the anchor that keeps you grounded. It is easy to forget your family while you are busy working overseas, but keeping in touch with them while away will give you a good feeling and strengthen your purpose of working in the first place. It is important to talk to your spouse and children while you are away. This might seem like common sense, but there is a great tendency to ignore the family when you are under high pressure at work. You can inform them about your day, your successes and failures and your frustrations and they are there to listen to you and provide you with some comfort and encouragement. That is why we have families to love and be loved. Their support is crucial for us to succeed in our careers and vocation.

However, please note that the above-mentioned advice is for ideal and normal families. This might not be the case for everyone. In that case, you need to avoid contacting them and putting them under stress. Instead, you should find a friend to keep in touch with while you are away from home.

Friends – "Friends in need are friends indeed." We've heard this phrase since our school days. Here, I refer to those very close friends who are friends indeed! Friends are a good source of entertainment, laughter, and relaxation. It is important to have a few good friends with whom you can talk , especially when you are under stress, and need a break from work. Usually, a call over WhatsApp or exchanging a few short messages, a little chit chat, can help you calm down and make you feel that there is a lot more to life than just work. It also helps you to relax by temporarily distracting you from the current crises or problems, focusing on humour or other interesting topics with your friends.

Sometimes, apart from personnel issues, you can discuss matters related to your own profession and well-being, to get their perspective and views on the matter. Friends are a great source to replenish your mental energy.

Silent moments – One personal practice that has always helped me to get back to the grind with more enthusiasm and energy is that of maintaining an hour or 40 minutes of silence. This is the time I am all by myself and my cell phone is switched off. I usually sit on the floor of my office or in my hotel room and just relax and feel all the thoughts running through my mind. It is some sort of meditation, and I might even pray for strength to move on. This practice has helped me a lot, and I wonder if you have tried to enjoy an hour, or 40 minutes completely to yourself to just do nothing and think of nothing. Try it if you haven't already and you will feel you have silenced your mind; it is like hitting the refresh button of your mind.

Many people I know and with whom I have discussed this practice say that they usually meditate for some time, which I believe is equally beneficial.

Find a mentor – Every great professional, accomplished millionaire and inventor had mentors. Consulting is a profession or trade that you learn from other people as well and blend with your own experience and skills. You are either mentoring someone or you are a mentee to someone. You can have one or more mentors and as a mentor, you can have one or more mentees.

A mentor can help you identify areas for growth and development and provide guidance and support as you work to achieve your personal and professional goals. They can provide guidance, insights and knowledge that can help you become an expert in a certain field. I have had very good mentors; a few of them contributed to my professional knowledge and others helped me meander through personal struggles in my career and family life.

As discussed, feedback is very important to improve your professional life. A mentor can give constructive feedback that can help you improve your skills and performance at work. They can help you to expand your network by introducing you to other professionals in your field of work, which can expand your network of contacts and help you grow in your carrier. They can provide you with guidance and support to develop and achieve your professional and personal goals.

Help people and give charity – Another way to look after yourself is to look after others. There is more pleasure in giving than in taking or earning. If you ask any millionaire, they will tell you that when they do charity, they feel much better than when they earn or take something from someone.

As human beings, it is in our nature to give. However, we are so absorbed in taking from others that we forget the pleasure of giving. Giving charity will give you the greatest pleasure and peace of mind.

That is why all religions in the world encourage charity. Whether you are religious or not, try giving charity to the poor and needy, especially those near and dear ones in your family or extended family. It will bring about a noticeable change; you will feel more peaceful and grounded.

Read – to be successful in life. You must read books. The choice of books and the way you apply that knowledge in your personal and professional life matter.

Warren Buffett spends 85% of his time every day reading newspapers and books. Bill Gates reads around 50 books a year; Elon Musk reads two books a day. Research carried out by Thomas Crowley, an author, speaker, frequent media contributor and founder of Rich Habits, mentions that 85% of self-made millionaires read at least two books a month. I cannot underscore the importance of reading books enough.

As a consultant, you are expected to be on top of things in all facets of your professional life. This means you will have to read books that generally help you have a better understanding of the world around you and build and sharpen your capabilities as an expert. Books will open your mind to new ideas, help you build new productive thought processes and widen and deepen your thought process which is essential for modern-day success.

Save money

"Beware of little expenses. A small leak will sink a great ship."

– Benjamin Franklin

As a freelancing consultant, your cash flow is cyclical if you are lucky, but usually, it is erratic and that is the truth. You must live with the fact that you earn a good sum of money in three months of a year; you may have to wait for six months to a year before you get your next assignment.

If you are a consultant from the south, you will be quite surprised to see that your colleagues in the north get work more frequently, because some are better than you, but mostly because they are from the north and the money comes to the donor from his country. This is very common in public-sector consulting. However, this is surely not the case in good consulting firms where contracts are awarded based on meritocracy, unlike public sector employers.

Regardless, you must be very good at managing your money. You need to save money for the rainy days when you have no work. Make sure you have life and long-term health insurance. If you happen to make a good amount of money, try to invest in a secure portfolio where you get a decent return on investment. I invested my money in real estate where I get a rental income.

Be very careful how you spend money. You should have a monthly expenses budget and over the year you need to save up for your annual family vacation. Spend money according to your budget and ensure that all expenses are recorded. While preparing your daily journal, make sure to reflect on your expenses; have you made reasonable purchases or are you being extravagant? Like all businesses, freelancing is a business and it is entrepreneurial in nature, which means you need to maintain your books of accounts.

Reflect but don't deflect

"Reflection in not an invitation to flagellate yourself for past failures. It's an opportunity to harvest the rich information embedded in your lived experience and use it to fertilize your future."

– Ryder Carroll

This quotation is profound, and it sets the principle for reflection. It is important to reflect because it gives you space to understand your words and actions, why you said what you said and why you did what you did. There is no other time you can have this conversation with yourself except in the process of reflection. This process will give you insights that will make you do and say things that will make you more effective and impactful in your personal and professional life.

If you follow the process of reflection, planning and action in your consulting practice, you will benefit hugely. It will help you improve your work by leaps and bounds. However, there is a catch! You need to undertake this process honestly, or else you will fall into the trap of deflection. Our mind has this tendency to justify a wrong as right and until we can call a spade a spade, we will never gain the correct insight, learn useful lessons and plan and improve our future actions and interactions.

Reflection is not so much about dwelling on your failures in your assignment as much as it is about understanding and examining your experiences to plan a better future.

Surfing The Net

Surfing the net is a good habit if you do it with a purpose and have set out an objective to be met within a certain time frame. Or else it is a time-wasting activity. Before you surf the net, ask yourself why you want to do so. Then, take a piece of paper and write down what you want to look for so that you don't stray away from your objective. Make sure you find what you need, one by one, and ensure that you are working with a time box you have organized for each item you plan to search. You need to take your usual break to refresh your mind so that you remain focused.

The ability to surf the net and acquire the information you need within a specific time period is important to collecting secondary data. Be patient, so that you remain on track till you have eventually collected the information. Do not forget to record the source of your information, which will be required in your report. Data and information mentioned in your report, especially secondary data, are useless without mentioning the source to your clients and colleagues.

Open Your Mind with a Fork and Spoon

We often judge people with a closed mind. You need to judge people less and try to understand them before judging them. The best way to open your mind about others is to share a meal or go out for lunch with them, so you can just eat and chat. You will understand them better and they may even be your colleague in another big assignment. This will help to build a collegiate bond and respect and appreciate one another. Having a meal together is one of the best ways to build a relationship. Even enemies become friends over a meal, or else one of you turns up dead!

Dress Code of a Freelance Consultant

Mary Lou Andre in her book *Ready to Wear – An Expert Guide to Choosing and Using Your Wardrobe* writes:

"*Your appearance at work can affect your career. Business is about communication, and your clothing is an important way to get your message across. It might seem unfair, but how you present yourself at work does speak volumes about your all-round professionalism.*"

The dress code for a consultant can vary depending on the type of consulting work they are doing and the specific company or client they are working for. However, there are some general guidelines that consultants can follow to dress appropriately for their work:

- Most consultants are expected to dress professionally, which typically means wearing business attire such as a suit, dress pants or skirts, dress shirts, and dress shoes. However, in public sector consulting, where you are visiting farms, rural areas and government offices, your choice of attire can be formal, but slightly toned down compared to private business consulting.

- You will have to pay attention to detail. Make sure that your clothes are clean, ironed and well-fitted. Please avoid wearing clothes that are too tight, too loose, or wrinkled.

- Dress appropriately for the occasion. In certain situations, you may be required to wear formal or casual clothes, so it is important to adjust your dress code accordingly. For example, if you are working with a startup, it may be more appropriate to wear a casual outfit when compared to a more traditional corporation. In rural development work, if you are on the field, you can generally dress casually, but when attending a government meeting, the dress code is semi-formal. I remember working on a project in the Maldives, where the government offices in Male and the residential island offices had a strict formal dress code, which they expected the consultants to follow as well. It meant wearing a necktie in the thick of summer!

- Avoid wearing flashy or distracting accessories, jewelry or watches that may draw attention and distract others from your professional appearance.

- Always follow the company or client's dress code. Sometimes, companies or clients have their dress code which they expect the consultants to follow. To present a professional image for these clients it is better to follow their guidelines and dress code.

Your Legacy Will Haunt You

The legacy of a consultant is shaped by their ability to make a positive impact and contribution to the organization and individuals they work with, both during a mission/engagement and after, for years to come. Some of the areas where consultants can build a legacy are as follows:

Enhanced strategic thinking:

One of the most valuable contributions a consultant can make is to help clients develop better strategic thinking skills. By working closely with their clients, analyzing their industries and organizations, their internal strengths and competitors and business processes, consultants can help their clients develop more effective strategies to meet long-term objectives.

Transfer of knowledge:

Successful consultants not only come in to solve problems and provide solutions to clients. They also build the capabilities of clients to continue to improve over time. This legacy of the consultant can be measured through the skills and knowledge the clients have retained and leveraged long after the consultants have left them.

Improved organizational performance:

Consultants are brought in by clients to facilitate change and improve a specific organizational goal. A successful consultant will leave behind a legacy of improved organizational and individual performance, whether that is translated in terms of higher revenue, greater efficiency, improved customer satisfaction, or in the case of public sector projects, the satisfaction of the administrators of the respective government ministry or parastatal.

Look Back, Smile and Give Yourself a Pat on the Back

Looking back and smiling about one's professional achievements is important for several reasons:

Celebrating your progress: Reflecting on your achievements and accomplishments can help you celebrate the progress made in your career. Celebrating your achievements, even the small ones, can be incredibly motivating and helps to provide a sense of purpose and direction.

When you look back on what you have achieved, it will give you a sense of confidence and self-belief. It is easy to get bogged down by your day-to-day challenges at work, but by taking a step back and looking at what you have achieved, it can be a great way to build confidence and encourage yourself to keep pushing ahead.

Perspective: Reflecting on your professional achievements from a distance can give you some perspective. You can get caught up in the minute details of your daily professional life, but by looking back, you will be able to see the bigger picture and understand the importance of milestones and successes that you might have overlooked at the time they were achieved.

Gratitude: Finally, by looking back and smiling about your professional achievements, you can cultivate a sense of gratitude for the opportunities and experiences that have come your way. Expressing gratitude and being mindful of your successes can help to foster a positive outlook and appreciation for the many blessings in your professional life. I thank God every day for giving me the opportunity to travel around the world and work in different countries and communities.

Chapter 8

Conclusion

I know by now you feel that you already knew most of the things written in this book. If you have this feeling, it's not bad. If you feel I have opened your eyes to something new, then it is even better. Please have an open mind and be positive always. Continuously learn and proactively build your skills and knowledge. Don't wait for your company or organization to invest in your learning.

Freely and generously share your knowledge with your colleagues, this will make you stronger as a person and people will like working with you. Always make time for your colleagues, reach out to those who are struggling with a piece of work and lend a helping hand.

Even if your clients or colleagues dislike you, or go against you, do not at any time give up or move away from the values you and your company stand for.

The client's confidentiality is of utmost importance. A personal example to share: A client blamed me and spoke disparagingly about my work to my colleagues, but I kept my mouth shut and didn't make any attempt to defend myself. In fact, his words were so harsh that one year later, after the completion of my assignment, when I was still in their country, the client told my team leader who was visiting them for another piece of work, that I was a persona non-grata in their country. I left the next month. It was a harsh thing to say, but the two people who had said this were not professionals and had a low capacity to deliver. I know both of them very well. Their entire comment was driven by religious bigotry. When my report was sent by the donor to their experienced experts, they found that my work met international standards, and was the best advice given to the client country.

The moral of the story: You will always win if you stick to your values. Never speak badly or challenge your clients aggressively. I learned this from other great consultants.

If your clients disagree with your recommendations or decide to ignore your guidance, step away politely and let the client do what they want to do. This way, you will maintain a good relationship with your client without compromising on your values. You must always work for the best interests of your clients. This will make you not only a good consultant but a great one!

As the saying goes, "Freelance Consultants don't fall from the sky." They have a history and a back story, which is more than their face value, rumours in the grapevine, or beyond your imagination. Never judge other consultants by their race, colour, religion, citizenship, the elite companies they might work for, or their attire, but judge them based on their values, professionalism, competence and how much they can work for the best interests of their clients. If you do this, they will in turn judge you in the same way.

Best wishes to all of you in becoming good human beings and great freelance consultants.

Let's get in touch – Ciao!

My Reference List is Your Reading List

1. Austin Kleon (2014), *Show Your Work! 10 Ways to Share Your Creativity and Get Discovered*, Workman Publishing Company, New York.
2. Barbara Minto (2009), *The Pyramid Principles – Logic in Writing and Thinking*, Pearson Education Limited, Essex, UK.
3. Bernard Garrette, Corey Phelps, and Olivier Sibony (2018), *Cracked It! How to Solve Big Problems and Sell Solutions Like Top Strategy Consultants*, Palgrave Macmillan, Switzerland.
4. Calvert Markham (2019), *The Art of Consultancy – A powerful Toolkit to Becoming a Top Consultant*, Legend Business Limited, London.
5. Dale Carnegie (2004), *Public Speaking for Success – The Complete Programme*, Manjul Publishing House, New Delhi.

6. Honoree Corder (2019), *You Must Write a Book,* Honoree Enterprises Publishing

7. Jacqueline Brassey, Aaron De Smet, and Michiel Kruyt (2022), *Deliberate Calm – How to Learn and Lead in A Volatile World, McKinsey Company Inc.* Harper Collins Publishers, New York.

8. Felix Haller (2020), *Awesome Emails – 10 Email Principles to Improve Your Communication and Accelerate Your Careers,* Amazon Publishing and Amazon.in

9. Gopika Kumar (2028), *Personal Power Equation + Step by Step Blue Print to Magnify your Image – The Ultimate Book on Personality Development, Communications and Soft Skills Enhancement,* Amazon. in.

10. Jim Loehr and Toney Schwartz (2003), *The Power of Full Engagement – Managing Energy, Not Time, Is the Key to High Performance and Personal Renewal.* The Free Press, New York.

11. Kam Kinght, *Speed Reading – Learn to read a 200+ Pages Book in 1 hour,* CPSIA USA.

12. Nir Eyal and Julie Li (2019), *Indistractable How to Control our Attention and Choose Your Life,* Bloomsbury Publishing, London

13. Marcus Buckingham (2022), *Love plus Work,* Harvard Review Press, Boston, Massachusetts.

14. Marrcus Aurelius (2023), *Meditation – Translated by George Long,* Finger Print Classics

15. Mary Lou Andre (2004), *Ready to Wear – An Expert's Guide to Choosing and Using Your Wardrobe, A* Perigee Book, The Berkley Publishing Group, A division of Penguin Group (USA) Inc.

16. December 6 (2022), *The State of AI in 2022 – and a Half Decade in Review –* McKinsey Global Survey

17. Paul Leonardi & Tsedal Neeley, *The Digital Mindset – What it Really Takes to Thrive in the Age of Data Algorithms, and AI,* Harvard Business Review Press, Boston, Massachusetts.

18. Ryder Carroll (2018), *The Bullet Journal Method – Track Your Past, Order Your Present, Plan Your Future,* 4th Estate - An imprint of Harper Collins Publishers, London, UK.

19. Sonke Ahrens (2017), *How to Take Smart Notes – One Simple Technique to Boost Writing, Learning and Thinking – for Students, Academics and Nonfiction Book Writers,* Create Space, USA.

20. Steven Pressfield (2022), *The War of Art – Break Through the Blocks and Win Your Inner Creative Battle,* Amazon Publishing.

21. Taiago Forte (2022), *Building a Second Brain – A Proven Method to organize Your Digital Life and Unlock Your Creative Potential,* Profile Books Limited, UK

22. Tony Buzan (2002), *Mind Map – The ultimate thinking tool that will change your life,* Harper Collins Publishers, London, UK.

Acknowledgement

This book would not have been complete in this form without the tireless effort made by my editor Mr. Anish Baskar. I would like to thank my Publishing Manager Mr. Barath Raj Muthukumar for organising everything that is required in the processes of publishing. His timely inputs are highly appreciated. I would also like to thank the publishing team of Notion Publishing in India. Finally, thanks to all my clients and colleagues and authors in the craft of writing who motivated me to write this book.